GRETCHEN and NICK

A "Bonnie and Clyde" Story for Today!

By
Max Call

published by
ACCLAIMED BOOKS
P.O. Box 18186
Dallas, Texas 75218

First Printing, 1988

For Lisa – Thanks for your forgiveness.

For the miracle of Justin Daniel.

For Jesus Christ for making it all possible.

CONTENTS

CONTENTS

INTRODUCTION

*"A friend loveth at all times,
and a brother is born for adversity."*

Proverbs 17:17

When I met Gretchen and Nick Barbetta, and heard them share their Christian witness, I knew God had blessed me by bringing us together. I could see our Lord Jesus in their eyes and I could hear His dear voice in their words. They were alive with God's Son and filled with the beauty of the Holy Spirit. Leaning back, I marveled at the glory they represented in the light of His unfailing love.

God had shown me a miracle. He had taken two fallen individuals and lifted them up to serve Him. He had redeemed all their sins and given them the gift of wisdom to use their life experiences to reach others who had fallen away.

Gretchen and Nick can speak the redeeming language of a lost generation because they were part of it. They can speak and teach with authority because they've faced the same challenges, trials and defeats. They can speak of victory over Satan because they have claimed that victory for themselves. They can speak the truth from the depths of their hearts because they have lived all the lies and found the truth that is available to all who ask.

This book is about the love God wants everyone

to share with Him. He gave Gretchen and Nick that love for each other in the very beginning and used it to draw them to Him. Let their inspiration become yours as you read their story.

In the name of Jesus,

Chaplain Ray

8

PROLOGUE TO MADNESS

> *"Our hour is marked, and no one can
> claim a moment of life beyond what
> fate has predestined."*
>
> Napoleon Bonaparte
> (1769 - 1821)

In the course of every person's life, a moment of truth must be faced. Nick and Gretchen built their life together on an addiction to heroin. They accumulated a vast fortune, only to see it fade away to their addiction. Like Napoleon, they had nothing left but life itself and they no longer had any control over that. All that remained was the love God had given them for each other. Their fates were sealed and there was nothing they could do for themselves to add a single minute to the time they had left. It was totally out of their hands. They had defeated themselves and were ready to give up in despair when the Father of the love they possessed showed them they had never been alone.

God had been with them all along the way, but just as Napoleon did before them, they felt defeated and lost until they learned the truth. When Napoleon faced his moment of truth, his victories were gone. He was no longer Emperor of France, and his vast fortune had vanished. He had become addicted to victory, just as many people become addicted to drugs. But as it is with a drug addict, he eventually became aware that a victory/fix did not produce the

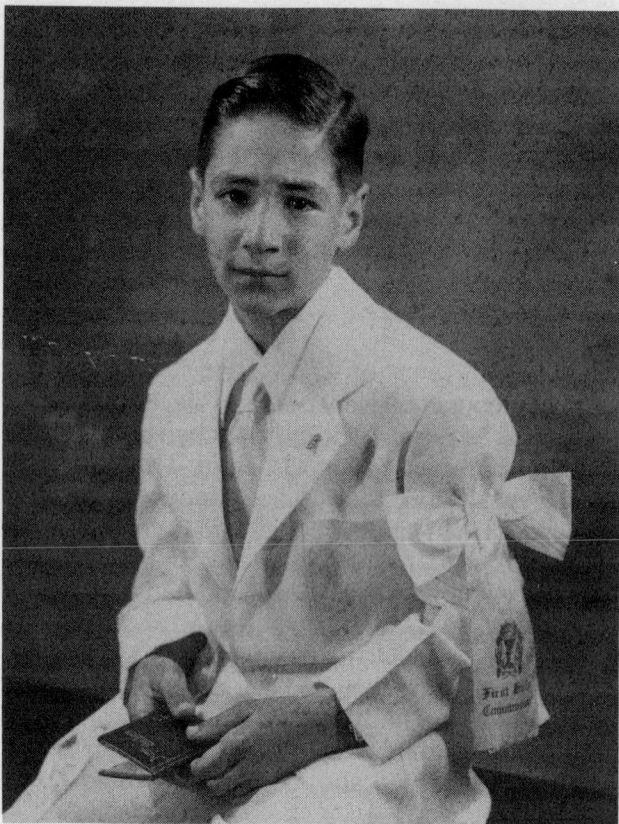

Nick Barbetta
My First Communion
May 14, 1950

lasting happiness and satisfaction it seemed to promise. All that survived his violence was the love God had given him for France. At least that could not be destroyed by his final defeat. It was the same for Gretchen and Nick.

Nick Barbetta was born on February 7, 1943 in Philadelphia, Pennsylvania. He was raised in the town of Bristol, a suburb of Philadelphia. His parents didn't agree on many things and it seemed to Nick that his father, Fred, was seldom home. They were both in their early twenties and both attractive. Fred's macho attitude toward women, especially his wife, Fannie, was partly due to his good looks and military service during World War II. He was a proud, independent man, but the fact that Nick was an only child in this Roman Catholic home speaks volumes about the love his parents shared in the early years of their marriage.

As a growing boy, in keeping with the family's Catholic tradition, he attended St. Anne's parochial grade school. Around children his own age, he was a "loner", stemming from the loneliness he felt at home. Traditionally, he was confirmed in the Roman Catholic faith as part of his school training. He readily admits, however, that he didn't understand the catechism and received no satisfaction from his confirmation. It was all simply tradition to him, nothing more.

"It had no importance at all for me," Nick recalled. "God was just a vague image to me and far removed from my thoughts."

Nick's father, after working at several other jobs, tried his hand as an able-bodied seaman in the Merchant Marine early in 1957. Following this, he obtained employment at the Miami International Airport. Nick and his mother moved to Florida sometime in late 1957 or early 1958. Fred liked Florida and eventually joined the Hollywood police

11

above—
Gretchen
with her
father and
mother,
Harry and
Madeleine

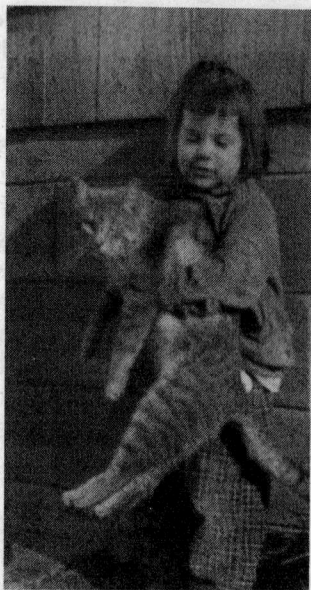

right—
Gretchen
was a
"Daddy's Girl"

force. Nick, however, hated living in Florida. He felt even more alone, and totally out of place. He knew no one and there weren't any relatives around to help him get acquainted.

Going to school didn't help. He found it extremely difficult to make friends and was constantly standing on the outside of school activities with no prospect of ever getting in. He was 15, just beginning to feel the pull of his manhood, when they made the move. Uncertain of his status in life, he retreated further into his shell of loneliness. The tension between his parents didn't help. It only added to his deep feeling of isolation.

At this time, Gretchen was only four years old. She was born in Highland Park, Illinois on March 9, 1954. Her father, Harry Martz, was in his fifties, a veteran of World War I with a mustard-gas disability. Her mother, Madeleine, was 14 years younger. She was the one in the family who had to work. Madeleine augmented his small disability pension with a full time job that kept her away from home for long hours.

In addition to Gretchen, there was a step-brother, Byron, 17 years older. Her sister, Harree, was only eight years older. They managed to live together, but their age differences prevented them from sharing many of the same interests. On the recommendation of her father's doctor, the family moved to Fort Lauderdale, Florida in 1960. She was six years old with no friends or playmates her age and upset about the move.

"I hated Florida," she said. "The only thing that made it bearable was the great amount of time that I could spend with my dad. Mother was never around because she had to work, and my sister was jealous of the attention I was getting from our father. The situation just wasn't very good between Harree and me."

13

Except for the times when he was in the V.A. Hospital for treatment, Gretchen's father was always on hand to give her the comfort and affection that every little girl loves to receive from her parents. Gretchen was the baby of the family, and he doted on her, and was always free to play with her.

In the absence of their mother, Harree had to assume many of the normal household duties. This included looking after Gretchen, but Harree couldn't overrule her father. She tried to be a *mother-figure* for her little sister while lacking a mother's authority.

Gretchen's half-brother, due to his age, was beyond the normal family squabbles. In many respects he was like his father in the brotherly affection he showered on his baby half-sister. As a result, Gretchen was given the attention and praise she desired from the two older men in her young life. Her father's love was the more important of the two because he was always available. From this, she assumed that an older man's love was more meaningful, dependable and satisfying.

Early in 1963, the health of her father began to decline dramatically. Gretchen had seen him go from good to bad before, but each time a stay at the hospital seemed to restore most of his vigor. She wasn't prepared for his death when it occurred later that year. Her whole life had been built on her father's love, and suddenly that love was no longer there. She was still too young to fully understand the true nature of her father's illness, so when he passed away, she subconsciously felt betrayed. He'd gone away and left her. Gretchen felt totally alone and neglected. She mentally crawled inside herself, secretly resentful of what God had done to her. She was only nine years old, but she was certain that real love could only come from an older man.

From childhood, Gretchen was gifted with superb feminine grace and physical coordination. She was a

14

pretty girl with the promise of becoming a very beautiful woman. Her childhood fantasies and daydreams often centered on becoming a famous actress. In her fantasies, she was always the center of attention and adoration. With her father gone, this dream couldn't be realized at home, and her self-imposed isolation at school didn't permit it to gain the slightest reality at school. As a result, she began losing interest in school, and rebelled against the discipline required to get an education.

With her mother working during the day, and her sister not really caring, she soon learned to fake being sick. This permitted her to stay away from school, and even when she was forced to attend classes, she found it easy to cut and run. There was, however, one bright spot in her young life.

At the age of 10, she discovered the joy and satisfaction of ice skating. Her beauty and coordination caught the attention of a skating teacher at the local ice rink. Mrs. Eddy had been a world-class figure skater herself and she saw the potential of a great skater in Gretchen. For two years, Mrs. Eddy coached Gretchen and encouraged her to think of winning in Olympic competition.

Gretchen responded to this praise and encouragement. Her talent was developing rapidly and held the promise of skating greatness. She was ready to make the necessary sacrifices to prepare herself for international competition. Mrs. Eddy warned her about all the work and training it would take, but Gretchen felt an Olympic Gold Medal and the glory that came with it, was worth whatever it took to be a champion.

She became possessed by this dream. Gretchen felt it was within her grasp. She could see herself standing on the high platform as the National Anthem was played and the American flag was hoisted on the high, center pole. While dreaming of

15

**A Skating Teacher saw Olympic Talent
in Grethen's skating.**

bowing her head and receiving the gold medal, she knew the whole world would be aware of her beauty and grace. The whole dream turned to dust when the only ice skating rink in Fort Lauderdale closed due to economics. The vast majority of people simply didn't think of ice skating while living or visiting in Florida. The rink couldn't compete with sunshine and beaches.

Feeling the loss of this dream, Gretchen failed to pass the ninth grade. She had never been interested in school and was too bored to keep up her studies. Her attendance fell off, so in hope of rekindling some spark of interest in learning, her mother enrolled her in a different school. Madeleine drove her to Hollywood five days a week throughout the academic year, but it didn't change Gretchen's attitude.

"Mother would let me out in front of the school," Gretchen confessed, "and I'd have some other drop-out friends waiting for me in back. They were all older than me. I was only 14 and the youngest of them was 17. I'd been smoking reefer and running with older kids since the rink closed, so it was only natural that I'd seek the company of those who were doing the same."

At this time, Nick was 25 and holding down the key disc jockey slot at Miami's number two radio station. His nighttime show pulled the highest ratings and he was a master at using *hard-rock* music to influence the activities of his large, youthful audience. He loved the music himself and knew how to present it with a special relish that delighted his avid fans.

Nick's life up that point had been one of self-indulgence. He'd starting drinking before his family moved to Florida, stealing his grandfather's home-made wine or finding older men to buy beer for him and his friends.

"It was easy," he explained. "We'd get some old street alcoholic to buy several quarts for us by letting him keep one for himself. Drinking was the only way I

17

could overcome my introverted feelings. Being drunk gave me the courage to do the things I wanted to do."

At the age of 12, Nick stole the car of a friend's father, and drove her and her boyfriend up to New York City over the Christmas and New Year's holidays. They slept in the car on the streets of Brooklyn, surrounded by violence. The excitement stimulated him and he craved more.

"It was scary and thrilling at the same time," he confessed. "We weren't drinking then because it took what little money we had with us just to eat. The excitement was all the 'high' I needed to enjoy myself.

"The police finally took notice of us," Nick admitted with a grin, "when the girl and her boyfriend were having a hassle on the sidewalk beside the car. Although I looked sixteen, I couldn't come up with a driver's license or any identification, so they hauled us in and called our folks."

Charges were never filed against Nick for any of this adventure, but when his father and mother showed up to get him out of jail, he concluded that his dad would hang around home more often if he continued to run away. This childish assumption made sense to him at a time when he felt neglected and unloved. Nick went back to Pennsylvania feeling certain he'd found a way to keep his father home. Although it didn't work out that way, he was convinced it did.

Nick did a lot of heavy drinking while he continued in school, and when he finished high school, he joined the Navy where he added narcotics to his habit.

"I was already into drinking pretty good when I went into the service and that's how I met Pete. He turned me onto *reefer*. I didn't quit drinking at first, but I quickly learned not to mix *reefer* with liquor. Little by little, I let the drinking go and turned to other things. In addition to *reefer*, I got into pills, codeine,

18

cough medicine and things like that.

"I was sailing high, wide and handsome when I married my high school sweetheart. She didn't share my fondness for chemicals, but I thought our marriage was made in heaven. I was still in the Navy when our daughter was born, but I had sea duty and our marriage went downhill fast. I'd married her out of loneliness, but when Lisa was born in 1965, we managed to stick together for a few more years."

When Nick was once more a civilian, he got involved with a crowd at the *Four O'Clock Club* in Fort Lauderdale. These people were tied into organized crime and that's where Nick plugged into a much heavier scene. He started dealing in a small way, enough to maintain his own habit and make a little profit on the side, but the real appeal of the club was in the violent action it provided. Nick had discovered the excitement he could create within himself through sadistically hurting other people.

"I loved it," he confessed, "and I never missed an opportunity to express myself by giving pain to others. One night at the club, I was high and looking for excitement. I knew I'd feel wonderful if I could just hurt somebody. This Englishman made himself available by not getting out of my way as I walked down the bar looking for an empty stool."

Nick asked the man to move out of the way, but the response wasn't fast enough. Hatred thickened Nick's voice as he shouted, "Okay, buster, we'll go outside and I'll teach you how to move faster."

He and one of his buddies were halfway to the door when the Englishman growled, "It'll be a pleasure to trim this Yank down to size."

I'm going to bust you up real good," Nick promised as they faced each other in the club's parking lot. Taking the first swing, he spun the Englishman around where his buddy could hit him with a hard right cross that pointed him back to Nick.

19

"Oh yeah!" Nick yelled, "I like this." Getting blood on his hands made him feel great.

Nick and his friend beat the Englishman into a bloody pulp. Thinking they'd killed him, they threw him under a parked car. As they were swaggering back toward the club, the man moaned in agony. Going back to finish the job, they suddenly changed their minds as they pulled him out from under the car.

"This isn't right," his buddy said. "This guy needs a doctor. We'd better call a cab and send him to the hospital."

A cab was called, but the driver refused to get involved. The police were called, however, and they took charge of the victim while Nick and his friend melted into the gathering crowd. No one knew anything about what happened and no arrests were made. To this day, Nick doesn't know what happened to the Englishman after he was released from the hospital.

"It was just something we could laugh and joke about," Nick recalled, "my buddy and I would pop a couple of pills, have a few drinks, and boast about the *number* we did on the poor slob."

Nick's memory of everything that happened at the *Four O'Clock Club* is clouded by a narcotic haze, but he does remember having a friendly conversation with a local radio personality one night over a few drinks. Halfway through their visit the man remarked on the quality of Nick's voice.

"Nick," he advised, "you should go into radio with a voice like yours. You could make good money and the work isn't too difficult. You'll need a broadcast license from the F.C.C., though."

"How do I get a license?" Nick asked.

"Like I did," the man replied. "There's a broadcast school up in Minnesota and they'll teach you all you need to know."

20

After getting the name and address of the school, Nick tucked it away in his wallet, promising to think about it, but not really intending to think too hard. Shortly thereafter, Billy Coppa, a friend and ex-con, got together with Nick and they decided to enjoy a little action. Billy was a big man, about 6'6", and in the vicinity of 350 pounds. He was a collector for some very heavy dudes in the area, and Nick's taste for violence made them seem natural partners. Billy enjoyed breaking arms and legs, and if that didn't get the results he wanted, killing also gave him pleasure.

"Billy and I left the *Four O'Clock Club*" Nick remembered, and we were driving up Interstate 95. At that time, it ended at Broward Boulevard and we were slowing down for the exit when another car pulled up alongside. They started shooting at Billy and I ducked down to the floor of the front seat.

"My brain was screaming, *Nick, you're gonna get taken out of here and you really don't know what's coming down.* I was scared and thrilled at the same time, but decided to check out the broadcast school and get out of town for awhile."

Taking his wife and daughter with him, he went north and completed broadcast training. When he left Minneapolis, he had a first-class broadcast engineer's license and the promise of an announcing job with a small radio station out on the Florida Keys. This was a major turning point in his life. Everything went smoothly until Nick started using heroin, and his wife didn't like it. She wanted out of his life.

"Taking Lisa with her," Nick said, "she left me and returned to the bright lights of my old hometown, Hollywood. She didn't file for a divorce, but she intended to make our separation one that I'd remember for a long time.

"The night I started at the Key West station, the man I was relieving at the console asked, 'What name are you using?'"

Nick hadn't given that a minute's thought and hesitated to answer. The man insisted that he needed a broadcast name to keep people from looking him up in the phone book and calling him at home.

"Hey," Nick finally replied, "maybe I should get an unlisted number."

"Naw," the older man answered with a wide grin, "pick a name that kinda fits your personality and you won't have to bother with none of that other stuff."

This made sense to Nick. He liked getting stoned all the time, so he figured it would be cool if he used a name that would fit his desired lifestyle.

"Before you leave the air," he suggested, "you can introduce me as Allen Stone. Maybe I can still keep my privacy and make that name famous as well."

"Now you're with it," the man concluded with a smile. "I'll give you the lead-in and you can take it from there."

So Nick Barbetta became Allen Stone. He was into all kinds of pills and pot, but had firmly resolved never to stick a needle in his arm. He had seen too many good men lose control of themselves with the needle and didn't intend to follow their example. He discovered it's one thing to make a resolution, but an entirely different thing to keep it.

"One evening, I was hanging out with a couple of pals and we put some money together, intending to buy a couple of pounds of reefer. One of them thought he knew where we could get some primo stuff, so we sent him out to make the buy. He was really proud of himself when he returned. In his opinion he'd lucked out and found some heroin instead. I immediately objected and refused to take the needle, but they kept pushing."

"Look, man," they insisted, "this is good stuff. It'll take you where you want to go and do it in grand

22

style."

"No way," Nick grumbled, shaking his head as they heated a couple of spoons and shot up while he just sat and watched. The pressure finally got to him and he stuck out his arm. "Okay," he growled, "hit me."

"Right on!" one of them exclaimed while the other tightened a belt around Nick's arm just above the elbow. The needle was ready. Finding the vein, he shoved it in. That was Nick's first hit and was all it took to start his love affair with heroin. This was what he'd been looking for in all the drugs he'd taken. It made everything else seem like child's play and he instantly knew that the 'big H' was going to become an important factor in his life.

During the next few months, Nick replaced his wife and child in his life with a growing love affair with the needle. If he couldn't get heroin, he still wanted to use the needle. To this day, he carries a scar on his arm where it abcessed from an injection of sleeping pill solution. His addiction became so strong that he was powerless to resist his desire for the needle.

"I wanted to mainline the real stuff," he admitted, "and one day I simply didn't make my shift at the station. I knew heroin was easier to obtain in Miami, so I packed my stuff and left Key West without saying anything to anybody."

Having graduated with a first class radio license from the Brown Institute of Radio & Television Broadcasting, Nick used the experience he'd gained to enter the radio community in Fort Lauderdale. As Allen Stone, he hooked on with the popular, number two, rock'n roll station in the nighttime disc jockey slot. He felt the power of the music and used it to reign over his young, impressionable audience. The moment young Gretchen heard his voice, something deep inside her stirred. She didn't understand it, but she knew she had to meet the man who could create such a longing in her heart.

She was running with a wild crowd, smoking dope and doing anything and everything that came into her head. Gretchen was no longer an innocent child; she was fifteen, going on thirty five, in the *fast lane*. She liked boys and knew how to interest them in doing whatever she enjoyed.

"One night," she recalled with a glint in her eyes, "a bunch of us were riding around, doing our thing, when I suggested that we go out to the radio station. They all agreed with me that it would be great fun to find out if the deejay would smoke some reefer with us.

"We pulled up to the station and I rang the doorbell, wanting the great Allen Stone to answer, but it didn't happen. He hadn't come on duty yet and two other guys opened the door. They seemed friendly enough, but none of us asked them to smoke anything even after they showed us around the station. We left and drove back into the city. On the way, we heard Nick, Allen Stone, start his shift at the microphone."

Later that night, Gretchen phoned the station and talked to Nick. She told him about her earlier visit, which he knew nothing about, and he didn't discourage her from trying again. When she hung up the phone, Gretchen knew what she wanted to do. Giggling to herself, she silently planned, *I'll go out and meet him tomorrow night, and I won't take so many people with me.*

Taking two older boys with her, she met Nick at the station, but neither of the boys had the nerve to ask him about smoking a little marijuana. Nick kept finding things to show this good looking little *chick*, just to keep her there.

Finally, as they were about to leave, Gretchen thought, *this is crazy.* She was halfway down the hallway toward the outside door when she turned

24

and faced Nick. "Look," she murmured, "do you want to smoke a joint with me?"

"Sure," Nick answered with a wide grin. "I'd be a damned fool to pass up a treat like that with such a fine looking woman."

Gretchen was only 15 and Nick was eleven years older, but his answer delighted her and when he held his lighter to her joint, the love he saw pouring from her big green eyes delighted him. It was love at first sight and neither of them denied its power. As they faced each other, God blessed them with a love they couldn't kill with drugs, violence or crime.

Nick with his mother, Fannie, and Fred, his father

A LOVE OF SELF-INDULGENCE

"The ability to make love frivolously is the difference between human beings and wild beasts."

Heywood C. Broun
(1888 - 1939)

With Nick, Gretchen found the love she lost when her father died. Madeleine loved her, but earning a living didn't leave her enough time to fill the void left by Harry's death. Unbeknownst to Gretchen, she was searching for the love of an older man. That was one strand of the unbreakable silken cord of love between Gretchen and Nick. There were other strands completely apart from her father.

Sleeping with Nick was giving her the security of his maturity, plus the beauty and excitement of their intimate relationship. For her, it was a match made in heaven, an answer to all her unspoken prayers, the fulfillment of all her dreams. She felt as if, by magic, reality had come to her most secret fantasies, and she reveled in Nick's love.

Their love affair was not a one-way street. Nick, too, was fulfilled in many ways. He knew this was no casual affair and was emotionally and physically satisfied. With his wife and daughter gone, he felt free to do as he wished without having to explain his actions to anyone. Gretchen, alone, possessed the unique ability to ease the pain in his heart and mind.

She responded to his caresses with total devotion and love. Her voice was like music to his soul and he accepted her as his life-partner, although he was still legally married to another woman.

There were many facits to the emotional bond between them. Gretchen was much younger than Nick, yet their lives contained many parallels. They both experienced great loneliness. They enjoyed the same type of music. Neither was reluctant to experiment with drugs. Nick hid his use of heroin from her, but they both used marijuana, pills and synthetic chemicals. Their inner hearts beat to the same drummer and they shared the same expectations.

As the number-one nighttime *radio-jock* in Fort Lauderdale, Nick made good money. He could afford to buy what they needed, but he'd been around the drug-bucket long enough to know where the dipper handle was located, so he started dealing.

"At that point in time," he explained, "I wasn't a dealer, but I always managed to get what we needed with enough left over to sell at a profit. This allowed me to support my heroin habit and Gretchen's needs without dipping into my own money."

Nick had always been withdrawn, a loner. When he used drugs, he was able to come out of his shell and express feelings he normally withheld. His feelings for Gretchen plumbed unused emotional depths. Heroin was the crutch that allowed him to reveal these new feelings. Nick felt free to dominate Gretchen with his love and she was able to accept this love by taking a secret pride in her submission to his strength. She was free to love him in return.

"The moment I met Nick." Gretchen remembered with a thoughtful smile, "I was very much impressed. I'd heard his voice over the radio and had a picture of him in my mind and I wasn't disappointed. He was tall, like I'd expected. With a name like Allen Stone, I really didn't expect his Italian good looks, but found

27

them exciting. His big brown eyes, broad shoulders and dark brown hair all helped give him a deeply romantic Mediterranean look that I adored.

"When I went home after meeting him, that first night," she added, "I was haunted by his eyes. Nick could send messages with his eyes and the message he was sending me wasn't one I could ignore. For me, his eyes were tender and soulful, happy and kind. However, I've seen Nick intimidate and manipulate others with just a glance."

Grinning with delight, Nick recalled his first impression of Gretchen. "As I opened the door at the station and saw her standing outside, flanked by two young men, I knew she was the girl for me. It was as if my most cherished dreams had come to life. She was the most beautiful woman I'd ever seen. Her eyes, as I appraised her, changed from grey to green and sparkled with excitement. When she smiled, my heart skipped a beat.

"I was 11 years older than her. She was only a couple of inches over five feet of perfectly carved femininity. The boys with her made no impression at all on me. I knew they were there, but my complete interest was captured by Gretchen. She was a delicate flower, just beginning to blossom, and I wanted her. Everything about her seemed to have a magnetic power that attracted me with a crushing need to know her better.

"Up to that moment, I'd never felt comfortable around strangers. In fact, I had always held something in reserve whenever I was in a social situation, but for no apparent reason I felt perfectly relaxed and at ease with her. Gretchen, just by the way she walked, talked and looked, made a captive of me.

"As I showed them around the station," Nick continued, "I kept trying to think of some way I could get to know her better. I was about to ask her for a date when she gave me an impish little smile and asked if I'd like to smoke a joint with her. That was the signal I was waiting for. It told me exactly what I needed to know. We were kindred souls, looking for the same thrills and excitement. I knew she wasn't using heroin as I was, and I resolved not to tell her of my growing addiction, but her willingness to smoke *reefer* put her on my wavelength and that was all that mattered."

Each of them, for different personal reasons, recognized the budding love that had been created between them, but this recognition was based on all the wrong reasons. Both were totally unaware that they'd been given a love that couldn't be killed. It was a love that went beyond the expectations stimulated by the physical attraction they shared for each other. It was a gift that neither of them had ever experienced before and they didn't have the slightest idea of where it came from or how it had been born. It was simply there for them to enjoy and they immediately claimed it without regard for what it actually represented.

Nick understood that Gretchen had been attracted to him, originally, by the sound of his voice and the music he put out over the air. His ability to use that music to set the mood of his listeners had drawn her to him, and the broad hints he'd made about getting high had given her the courage to think he might be interested in a little fun on the side while at work.

"Starting at the age of 12," Gretchen admitted, "I had been in rebellion against my mother's authoritative manner. I'd run away from home a couple of times, and on one such occasion, I'd gone out of state with some older boys. A guy who worked in a local drugstore, took me up to Atlanta with five other guys. We were only out to have a little fun, staying with his friend, Mark. His mother was a very tolerant woman and let us stay for about a week before she called my mother and the mother of one of the younger boys.

"The boy's parents came up to get us," Gretchen continued, "and I knew I was in trouble. Mom was a very religious person. My religious upbringing was entirely different from Nick's. Mother went to church regularly and she related her life to Jesus, but she didn't preach the gospel to me and I didn't know the Lord through anything she said. She simply expected me to know and to behave in a Christian manner, and that I hadn't done.

"When we got home from Atlanta, my mother had me sent to Juvenile Hall. She said it was for my own good, a lesson I needed to learn, but a week in Juvenile Hall didn't actually teach me a single thing. I still wanted to run. I still felt unloved. I was still angry at my father for dying and leaving me. This, however, was an anger I didn't really know I possessed or felt, but it did affect my life before I met Nick.

"Nick responded to my feelings and neither of us ever doubted that we were madly in love with each other," Gretchen murmured, fondly gazing at him. "And with that love, I no longer felt the need to rebel for the old reasons. All I wanted was to be with him, to love him and have him love me."

Gretchen's mother neither approved nor disapproved of Nick. She accepted him and the relationship he had with her daughter because it seemed to give Gretchen something that she needed and wanted. It also softened Gretchen's bitter, rebellious nature. When Madeleine met Nick, she saw how much older he was than her daughter, but he was working and wasn't a bum, so she tolerated their relationship.

She had always tolerated Gretchen's friends and allowed them to party at her home while she was at work or in church. Madeleine reasoned that if she kept them around, she might be able to reach them through prayer and informal sermonettes.

"All of my friends and I," Gretchen stated, "took advantage of mother's good nature. We partied in her

30

house, smoked dope, drank beer and messed around. Mother would come home and find kids laid out all over the place. She knew what we were doing and permitted it to happen just so she could preach to us. We even junked her house and she didn't complain too much. With Nick it was different. He didn't play around with kids and all my wild friends drifted away."

The love-birds had been hanging out together for about four weeks when they decided to take a little trip just to be together on their own. Nick, at Gretchen's suggestion, took her north to Atlanta where Gretchen knew they could stay with Mark and his mother, but Madeleine took a dim view of the jaunt. Gretchen was a juvenile and Nick was an adult. By taking her across the state line, he'd committed statutory rape and she obtained a warrant for his arrest. The warrant and charge was never pressed forward, but when they returned to Florida, Gretchen was threatened with another stay at Juvenile Hall.

"That was a threat that mother always kept over my head." she said, "but I never really took it too seriously. My first trip to the Hall didn't do much to improve my behavior and mother knew that as well as I did. The arrest warrant and charge was noted on Nick's police record even though it was never prosecuted to a conviction."

Shortly after this episode, Nick learned that Gretchen's mother had a small apartment in her back yard for rent. He wanted to be near Gretchen as much as possible, so he rented the place and moved in. This delighted them both and Madeleine voiced no strong objection. She hoped that by having them close, she might be able to influence their lives with a little Christian teaching.

Madeleine knew they were using some kind of drugs, but she didn't suspect, and wasn't aware of Nick's involvement with heroin or his dealing. At that time, even Gretchen didn't know about his heroin habit. She knew he was using something because she could see it in his eyes, but she didn't think he was on the needle. In fact, Nick had gotten a friend to buy him the cosmetics he needed to cover his tracks so Gretchen couldn't discover his secret.

Living in the back yard apartment, Nick would come home after his shift at the station to find her waiting for him. She would slip out of the house after her mother was asleep, and watch for him. Although Madeleine suspected this was happening, she didn't want to make a fuss, fearing Nick would leave and take Gretchen with him. Then she'd have absolutely no chance of reaching them with her teachings. Unbeknownst to either Nick or Gretchen, she had several members of her church's Bible study group praying for them, and firmly believed those prayers would be answered in God's time.

"I didn't know," Gretchen admitted, "that Nick was shooting up while he was on the air. Sometimes I'd borrow Mother's car and drive him out to the station and just hang around while he worked, but often he'd find some reason to get upset with me and send me home, so he could get a fix. Then, knowing I'd be listening on the car radio, he'd play a song that would tell me he was not really angry. In a way, our love affair was very public, but without knowing us, no one other than my mother was really aware of it."

The affair came to a head after a couple of months of Gretchen sneaking out to Nick every night. She finally told her mother, "Look, I'm tired of sneaking around and I think you know I've been sleeping with Nick, so I'm moving out back with him."

"Honey," Madeleine objected mildly, "it isn't right for you to live with him without being married. You're also too young for him, but there doesn't seem to be much I can do about it. You know I love you, and I like Nick, but I wish you'd give this a lot more thought before committing yourself to an open relationship."

32

"I love him and he loves me," Gretchen responded adamantly, "and that's all we need to live together. We don't need a piece of paper to make our love legal. All we need is each other, so that's the way it's going to be."

"Okay," her mother agreed reluctantly, "but just remember, you still have a room here in the house and you're not locked into a relationship that he can break if you do something that displeases him. Just be careful and don't get yourself messed up before you know he's committed himself to your well being."

In making that move, Gretchen broke the last vestige of her mother's parental control. Nick was pleased and nothing else mattered to her. She was with the man she loved. Having made the break, she began expanding her interests by going back to school to get her GED. Once this was accomplished, Gretchen enrolled in the drama program at a nearby community college.

Gretchen still didn't know that Nick was married and had a young daughter. She thought he was free of all obligations. Whenever he borrowed his wife's car for a few hours, he told Gretchen that it belonged to his sister. He never took Gretchen with him when he visited to spend a few hours playing with Lisa. If Gretchen had known about his family, it wouldn't have made any difference because it was too late for her. It was too late just ten seconds after they met, as far as Gretchen was concerned. She had fallen deeply in love with Nick and nothing could or would change that.

Gretchen was still vulnerable to feelings of guilt, constantly renewed by her mother, which led to further rebellion. She knew her relationship with Nick was not right and rebellion was the only way she could justify what they were doing.

"Mother never actually told me I was guilty of

violating God's law," Gretchen admitted, "but she was a past master at making me feel guilty. I resented it and in the back of my mind, I resolved, *If you think I'm being bad now, just wait and see what I do next.*"

After moving in with Nick, it didn't take long for Gretchen to become aware of his heroin habit. He would be uptight at times, yet after spending a few minutes in the bathroom with his dope, he would emerge in a very mellow mood. She also began suspecting that he was getting high at work on something he wasn't sharing with her.

"Yeah," Nick agreed, "I'd put that seven-and-half-minute record on the turntable, and while it was playing I'd wrap the belt around my arm and take a hit. I even hinted as much over the air, so it isn't surprising that Gretchen would suspect something was going on.

"Hey," he continued, "I loved playing my kind of music and I used it to influence the conduct of my listeners. I understood the beat and thrust of *hard-rock*. I was fully aware of how it was being used to lead rebellion against the establishment. I'd get my audience all steamed up and turn them on.

"One night, I got the phone number of the White House and put in a call to President Nixon. I wanted to bug him about Vietnam, but I was told the President wasn't available, so I put the White House phone number out over the air. I asked all my listeners to phone Nixon and tell him off. They tied up the White House switchboard for hours that night. A bunch of dope-heads was able to push Nixon's button because I knew how to use the music to turn them on."

As Nick's need for heroin increased, his on-the-air popularity continued to grow. His audience didn't know his real name or what he looked like, but they listened and fell for his drug-induced philosophy. He got deeper into dealing, always being extremely careful whom he dealt with and limiting his action to his immediate needs. He was at peace with himself about what he was doing because he still felt he was in control.

"In reality," Nick recalled, "I was very insecure and felt totally inadequate. I was over my head, doing things that were almost too wild to be believed. If I hadn't been strung out on heroin, I could have utilized my gifts and talents for a better purpose, but my insecurities held me back. The only way I could overcome my personal doubts and get on top of the situation was by doing a shot of dope."

"I was smoking dope and popping pills," Gretchen said, "but I wasn't getting any of the *peace* and *satisfaction* that I thought I saw Nick enjoying. My emotions were in constant turmoil, running from high to high and from low to low, so I dug in my heels and decided it was time for me to join him on the *trip* he was taking. I started looking for evidence of what he was doing so I could demand that I be included in his fun and games."

"She knew I was dealing heroin," Nick added, "but that's all she knew and I had promised myself that she would never stick a needle in her arms. I'd seen too many young girls turned onto heroin and then turned out as hookers to support their habits and that wasn't a fate I wanted, or would permit, to happen to Gretchen. She kept asking what I was on, but I wasn't about to tell her."

As it happened, however, Nick was soon given something else to think about. He spent a day in Miami, buying the dope he needed for his dealing, when suddenly everything fell apart and he faced his first drug-related arrest. It was 1971 when his girl-friend's mother blew the whistle on the leading disc jockey of the top *rock and roll* radio station in the Fort Lauderdale market.

Madeleine, Gretchen's mother, always stood by Gretchen and prayed for her.

BUSTED BY A
LOVING MOTHER

"The dignity of truth is lost with much protesting."
Ben Johnson
(1573 - 1637)

Nick was feeling great when he returned from
Miami. He'd made a good connection and everything
he needed for the next few weeks was safely tucked
away in the trunk of his car. Pulling into the long
driveway, he drove back to the apartment with a
satisfied grin on his handsome face. Gretchen was
standing in the apartment's open doorway to greet
him.

"You're back early," she observed. "How did it
go? Did you get what you wanted?"

He answered as he got out of the car. "It couldn't
have been better. My connection came through with
some good stuff that will take a good cut."

Walking to the doorway, Nick swept Gretchen up
in his arms and whispered, "I'll do the cutting before I
go to the station tonight."

Leaving the dope in the car didn't concern Nick.
An hour later, when he and Gretchen were unloading
the trunk, Madeleine called to them from the back
door of the main house. "Gretchen, I've got to go to
the store and I've lost my purse. Have either of you

seen it anywhere?"

Not me," Nick answered, "I just got back from Miami."

"I haven't seen it, Mother," Gretchen replied.

Can y'all come and help me look for it?" Madeleine asked as Nick carried his armload of dope into their apartment.

No, Mom," Gretchen yelled back at her. "I've got to help Nick get ready to go to the station. Just keep looking, I'm sure you'll find it."

Nick's a big boy," Madeleine responded, "I'm sure he can get ready for work by himself. Come and help me, please."

"Sorry, Mom, but he needs me," Gretchen shouted, following Nick inside and closing the apartment door behind her.

Suddenly, Madeleine was angry. Slamming her door, she marched back to the center of the kitchen, seething with anger and disappointment. She knew they were using drugs and could always use a little extra cash. There hadn't been a great deal of money in her purse, but there was enough to interest an addict. She felt justified in suspecting that her daughter might well know what happened to her purse, as Gretchen had been around all day. She'd even been in the house, doing her laundry. Madeleine kept looking for the purse, but as each minute passed, her anger grew stronger.

Without giving Madeleine's lost purse another thought, Gretchen helped Nick clear off the kitchen table and lay out his dope for cutting. Nick made a trip to the bathroom. When he returned, she knew he'd shot up. She could see it in his eyes as he started processing his heroin for resale. He cut it four times by sifting it through a nylon stocking into bowls on the table. Gretchen weighed it out and wrapped each batch in small waxed paper squares, neatly folded over into uniform-sized packages. Nick's gun was

38

also on the table where he could reach it quickly if they were interrupted.

It had been a good trip. He had also picked up some stolen credit cards and some blank money orders from a recent bank robbery in California. He was mentally spending the money he was going to make off this load and was feeling very good about everything.

Looking across the table at Gretchen, he smiled with satisfaction and suggested, "Let's go out and get something to eat. We can come back and finish the cutting and then I'll go to work."

"Okay," Gretchen agreed happily, "Let me brush my hair and fix my makeup and I'll be ready."

Indicating everything on the table with a wave of his hand, Nick said, "We'll leave this stuff out so we can get right back to it." As Gretchen headed for the bedroom, he added, "Be sure to bring your key so we can get back in when we return. I'll lock up while you're getting ready."

Madeleine, boiling with frustration and anger, watched them back their car down the driveway and disappear down the tree-lined street. Once they were gone, she took her keys and headed for the apartment, fully expecting to find her empty purse on their bed.

Entering the apartment, she was shocked by what she did find. The gun on the table told her that Nick was into some pretty heavy action, and she didn't want Gretchen caught up in something she couldn't handle. Going back to her house, she mentally debated what course of action she should take, but her anger was now tinged with fear for her daughter's safety, so she picked up the phone and called the police.

Gretchen and Nick enjoyed a cozy dinner. Both were in a good mood and very much at ease. Nick had the drugs he needed for the next couple of weeks and the prospect of making a little extra money was very good. They laughed and joked with their waitress at the restaurant and Nick left a generous tip on the table as they got up to leave.

Driving back to the apartment, he suggested they might get away for the weekend and have a little fun at the beach. This was typical of Nick when he was feeling on top of the world, so Gretchen knew that whatever he was using, it was working. She still couldn't visualize him sticking a needle in his arm, but her doubts were beginning to grow stronger. As he slowed the car and turned into Madeleine's driveway, she was startled by his sudden reaction.

"What's going on?" he exclaimed. "What's that cop doing on your mother's front porch?" Throwing the car in reverse, he quietly backed into the street. He'd seen the police car further down the driveway and immediately sensed the danger of arrest. The door to the apartment was standing open and he knew the police must have found the drugs they'd left on the kitchen table.

"Let's get out of here," Gretchen urged as he slowly pulled away, trying to avoid attracting attention. He wanted the cop to think they were strangers, simply turning around in the middle of the block.

Up to this point, Nick had sheltered Gretchen from the ugly reality of the drug scene. He had made all the contacts, and the dealing had involved only him. She had done none of the buying and had no direct connection with his activities. He also felt certain Madeleine wasn't about to tell the police that she allowed her 16-year-old daughter to live with an older man in her back yard apartment. After all, Madeleine was *church-people* and it wouldn't be like her to reveal their relationship unnecessarily. He wanted to know what was happening at the house and figured Gretchen could phone home and find out without too much hassle.

40

They headed straight for U.S. Highway 1. Suddenly, there were police cars everywhere. The Shell station at the corner was swarming with cops, so Nick cruised through the stop signal at the intersection without stopping. He was ready for a high speed chase, but it didn't happen.

At a friend's house, they parked the car out of sight and hurriedly went inside. Gretchen phoned her mother. Instead of answering questions, Madeleine asked a few of her own.

"Where are you?" she pressed. "When are you coming home?"

"We're just driving around," Gretchen answered, "and it'll be a little while before I get home."

After the phone call it was obvious that Madeleine expected them to return and she didn't say anything about the police, so Nick assumed that she wanted him caught. He was expected at the radio station and knew arrangements would have to be made for someone else to take his shift or the station would go off the air. Hoping to catch one of the other men by arriving as early as possible, he decided on the course of action he would have to follow.

Looking at his friend, he asked, "Jack, will you drive Gretchen home? I've got to get out to the radio station before anything more happens."

"Sure," Jack replied.

Turning to Gretchen, Nick instructed, "Go home and find out what the police are doing." She nodded her understanding as he added, "I'll call you from the station, so stay by the phone."

Nick arrived at the station just in time to start his shift. Before he could explain anything to the man he was relieving, Nick found himself alone. Hoping to catch the morning DJ and talk him into coming in, he started phoning all the guy's regular hangouts, but he came up empty. In desperation, he started announcing over the air between records that the

41

station owner's son had an important message at the station. Nick also knew if the police were listening, they'd know where to find him.

He could, of course, just walk off and let the station go dark, but that would have been a violation of his license and would have been totally unfair to his trusting employer. It was simply a case of being trapped until the man's son came in to get the message. While waiting, he screwed up his courage and called Gretchen. She answered the phone on the first ring.

"Nick," she half whispered, "the cops found everything! They've been all over the place and they're on their way out to the station!"

"Look, honey," he murmured, "I'm stuck here until Tom or somebody shows up. When did the police leave there?"

"About five minutes ago," she answered. "You better leave now!"

Just as Nick hung up the phone, Tom and a friend finally arrived, looking for the important message Nick had been broadcasting. They'd been drinking, but Tom wasn't too drunk to go on the air, so Nick laid his problem on the station owner's son.

"Tom, you've got to take over my show. The police are on their way out here to arrest me."

"You're kidding," Tom responded with a laugh. "They can't be coming for you. If they were, they'd already be here. Besides, you haven't done anything. I've been listening to your broadcast and there's no reason for any complaint."

"Man," Nick insisted, "I'm in big trouble. You haven't the slightest idea of what I'm into. Believe me, I've got to get out of here and you've got to keep the station on the air. If you won't, I've got no other choice but to run and let the signal go silent."

"Okay, okay," Tom finally agreed. "I'll take it for you, but if you're pulling my leg, you're going to learn what big trouble really means."

Tom took over the broadcast console and Nick headed for the station door. The transmitter and studio was located at the very end of a rural road, so when he saw the headlights of a car coming, he knew it had to be the police.

That must be the man, he thought to himself as he made a dash for his car. Climbing inside, he sank out of sight on the floor. He watched the lights outside the station's front door, and waited for the cops to appear at the door. Holding his breath, he watched the officers ring the entrance bell, and waited for Tom's friend to let them in. They thought he was Nick and barged into the station, announcing his arrest and reading him his rights. They closed the door behind them, as Nick hoped they would. Getting behind the wheel, Nick quietly started his car and took off. He had to find a place to stay. As he roared down the road he remembered friends who had a cottage on one of the Miami canals. They kept a boat out back, so if the police showed up there, he could get away over the water.

Nick tried slipping back to the neighborhood to touch base with Gretchen, but everytime he cruised by, the police were on hand. He knew he couldn't stay in hiding for the rest of his life and decided to call his father, who was now a detective on the Hollywood police force.

"Dad," he told him over the phone, "I'm in serious trouble."

"I know," his father replied. "Why don't you meet me somewhere and we'll talk it over. Maybe there's something you can do to help yourself."

"I'll meet you." Nick offered, "if you'll promise not to bust me. I don't want to be set up either, so don't promise and then have somebody else there to take me."

"You know I can't do that," his father said firmly.

"I'll do everything I can to help you, but I can't help you evade arrest."

"Then I can't meet you," Nick stated flatly and broke the phone connection.

Feeling totally stymied, Nick didn't know where to turn for advice or aid. He couldn't risk bringing Gretchen into the problem; she was still clear of any charges and he didn't want to get her involved. Sitting with him on the back porch of the canal house one afternoon, his friend, Pete, came up with an idea.

"If you're interested, Nick," Pete suggested, "I know an attorney that might be able to help."

"Call him," Nick urged. "Can he be trusted?"

"Yeah, man, this guy's been around," Pete said. "He's handled matters for a couple of guys I know and they swear by him."

The attorney was called and a meeting set up. Nick related everything to him and sought his advice. What the lawyer said seemed to make sense.

"Let's go down and turn you in," the attorney advised. "We'll bail you right back out and then we'll deal with whatever charge they give you. This is your first offense and I'm reasonably sure you'll only get probation, so let's get started and get all this behind you."

"Okay," Nick agreed.

"Good," the attorney bragged, "we'll have you back at work before your radio audience has even missed you."

"I'm not so sure the station will take me back," Nick said ruefully, "I don't think they can afford to have someone with a pending drug violation playing records for their station."

Following the lawyer's advice, Nick turned himself in, and while he was being processed, the attorney arranged bail. He was out on the street in less than two hours, with a court appearance scheduled for twelve months later. As he figured, his

44

broadcasting days were over, but he was free to do other things.

After getting back with Gretchen, Nick had to face the fact that he didn't have a job and he'd have to find another way of making ends meet. Since he was already dealing and had some good connections, he decided to get into the drug business in a bigger way. His needs still had to be met every day, so he didn't feel he really had another choice. Using the money he had left, he bought an inventory of narcotics, including heroin, and moved deeper into the growing drug culture.

By creating a small network of sub-dealers, Nick avoided doing business directly with the street addict. Everything he sold was delivered, on a cash basis, to only three men. They, in turn, sold to street pushers/users, but that wasn't Nick's concern. As his business grew, so did the business of his sub-dealers and Nick began to think there was no end to the money he could make and still not risk street arrest or a police trap. He picked his people, they didn't pick him, and he flatly refused to do business with strangers. Everything ran smoothly until the date of his trial.

His attorney told him repeatedly, that he would get a short period of probation and nothing more. Every time they discussed the case, Nick was assured he wasn't in serious trouble. He went to court with that idea firmly set in his mind, so when Gretchen asked if she should go to court with him, he turned her down.

"Naw, you stay here," he said. "I'll be home in a couple of hours. I'm going in to hear the judge's lecture and I'll walk out with a little probation." Kissing her cheek, he added, "We'll go out to dinner tonight and celebrate."

His lawyer met him at the courthouse, still oozing confidence and assurance that Nick would be back home in time for lunch. They looked like a couple of well dressed businessmen as they entered the court. Nick smiled at everyone, letting them know he had nothing to fear from the judge, but once the preliminaries were out of the way, things didn't go as planned. The newspapers were full of drug-related stories and the Florida legal system was facing an overflow of drug cases. It was bogged down with men, women, and even children appearing on narcotic violations. That morning, Nick's judge was fed up with what drugs were doing to the State's court. Nick's attorney deliberately presented a weak defense which gave the judge ample opportunity to vent his disgust.

"Mr. Barbetta," he stated grimly, "I'm not sure what I should do with you, so I'm going to lock you up indefinitely. You're of no value to society and you're dangerous to yourself, so I think it's time to put you away where you can do no harm to anybody." Rapping his gavel, he called a lunch break, saying, "We'll set your sentence after an hour's recess."

Nick couldn't believe his ears. He started to feel a little crazy. Walking out into the hallway with his lawyer, he grabbed the man's lapels and demanded, "What are you doing in there?" That man is going to lock me up indefinitely. Why are you letting him do that to me?"

"You're getting what you deserve," the man yelled back. "You're a junkie and you belong in jail! All I'm doing is letting the court serve the good people of Florida by putting you away!"

All of Nick's anger suddenly came to a boil. Gripping the lawyer's shirt, Nick drove his fist into the man's stomach. Taking a second punch at his chin, he backhanded the attorney's face and dropped him to the floor. The court bailiff grabbed him and hauled him off his victim as the lawyer screamed from the floor.

"I'll get you for this! I'm an officer of the court and

you're a dope pusher. I'll sue you for every dime you'll ever hope to make and see you locked up for a long time!" Nick could still hear him screaming and threatening as the bailiff led him away.

A few months after the trial, Nick discovered that his attorney and his father were involved in a dispute. The lawyer used Nick to get revenge for something Nick's dad had done to legally embarrass him in a previous case.

The relationship between Nick and his father had never been close. With Nick's drug involvement, there was little likelihood of that changing. His father knew what Nick was doing, but he didn't press the matter as long as it didn't directly concern the Hollywood police department. This was one of the primary reasons Nick was so careful in his dealings, but he wasn't aware of how his heroin addiction was beginning to affect his actions. There were times when Nick did foolish things because his mind was focused solely on his need for a fix.

As he waited for the court to reconvene for his sentencing, Nick's anger simmered down enough for him to appear normal. He wanted a fix, but there was no time or opportunity to arrange it. The District Attorney planned to call Gretchen's mother to testify against him and she was in the building. Nick was nervous about this prospect and considered it the cause of his unease.

When the judge called the court to order, Madeleine saw what was happening between Nick and his attorney. She was aware of the judge's opinion, and she didn't like the smug, self-satisfied attitude of the prosecuting attorney. Seeing that Nick was about to be railroaded into an unjustified sentence, she re-fused to testify against him. Her previous statements to the prosecution hadn't been made under oath, so when she said, "I'm sorry, your honor, but I really don't remember exactly what happened," the court had to accept it.

Because of this, the prosecution tried to make a big thing out of Nick's living with Madeleine's minor daughter. He stressed the great difference in their ages. He tried to imply that Madeleine's refusal to testify was a result of her own fear of being exposed as a mother who would permit her 15-year-old daughter to sleep with a drug addict in her own home. He even hinted at the possibility that both mother and daughter might be addicted themselves, and needed Nick's freedom to keep them supplied. This wasn't stated openly, but if it had been, Nick's attorney might have let it stand unchallenged.

All of this gave the judge time to do some thinking of his own, and at the conclusion of the trial he sentenced Nick to five years probation, beginning with an 18-month stint in the *Spectrum* drug rehabilitation program. At that time, *Spectrum House* was considered the answer to Florida's drug problem, but there were facilities in Ft. Lauderdale and Miami where *Spectrum* counselors used fear and humiliation as the motivating factor in their treatment.

The people assigned to them by the courts were stripped naked emotionally and then mentally *re-dressed* to *Spectrum's* specifications before being graduated back into society. Nick was willing to give the program a try until he saw and met the people in charge of his treatment.

48

WITHOUT REASON

"Is pride the never-failing vice of fools?"
                    Alexander Pope
                    (1688-1744)

Nick was assigned to the Miami *Spectrum House* to begin his 18-month treatment program. Upon arriving, he was interviewed by the intake officer, a civilian who had been in the program himself, and briefed on what he could expect. Nick had accepted the program to stay out of prison, but what he really wanted was to get back on the street and get high again. He missed Gretchen and didn't like the idea of such a long separation. The first question he asked caused the man to laugh.

"Look," he questioned, "when can I get out of this place?"

"You're the first person to come in here," the man chuckled, "and ask that question before you even get started. You're in here for 18 months, so just simmer down and relax. You've got a long ways to go before it's over."

As Nick settled into the routine, it became very apparent that he wasn't going to enjoy his stay. In addition to his withdrawal problem, he didn't like what he saw happening to the people around him. The assistant director of the house was an 18-year-old kid from New York who'd graduated from a program up there and been sent down to Miami. It was immediately obvious the kid didn't care for Nick and neither of them made any effort to hide their mutual animosity. In fact, the kid did everything he could to keep Nick on edge. He was certain that Nick was just playing a game and kept trying to goad Nick into betraying himself.

"So you like young girls," was his snide remark in their first session. "So do I, and I understand that you have a daughter who's about eight. I think I'll look her up and see if we can't get it together. Sleeping with your little girl would sure be fun!"

Nick knew that the guy was just trying to push his buttons, so he retorted, "I'm not going to be here long enough for you to get started with my daughter. Besides she's too smart to fool with a kid like you."

"Don't wise-off with me," the kid warned. "You won't be leaving here until I give you clearance, and you're a long way from that right now."

Chuckling softly, Nick leaned over the guy's desk and whispered, "When I decide to leave here, you'll look up and I'll be gone."

"Hey, man," the kid snarled, "I want you to go! I want to send you to prison where you won't ever be able to get next to another 16-year-old girl again. By the time you get out of prison, that little chick of yours will be old enough to do anything she wants without you." Looking Nick straight in the eye, he grinned viciously and hissed, "If she's into dope like you are, she'll probably be working the street and doing anything anybody tells her to do just to get a fix."

"Don't fret your little brain about any of that, Sonny," Nick growled in return. "You won't be sending me to prison because I'll have it all down pat when I decide to leave here."

Nick was older than most of the men and women in the program and he possessed the native intelligence to avoid many of the hassles that seemed to engulf some of the others. The house's policy of using fear of humiliation by making many men submit to having their heads shaved wasn't for him.

Adult men were forced to wear diapers for minor infractions of the house rules. Make-work projects, such as dusting the same piece of furniture for hours at a time, were often used.

Girls were not allowed to use any makeup, and had to wear stocking caps at all times. It wasn't unusual to see both men and women wearing signs that read, "Don't talk to me," or "I'm dangerous." Nick caught his share of these childish things, but his age and size saved him from a lot of embarrassment and humiliation. He knew how to play the game, and by rolling with the punches, he managed to control his explosive temper as the months rolled by.

About mid-point in his program, Nick and several others from the Miami house were sent up to the Fort Lauderdale facility for a *Spectrum* holiday. There were three houses up there and in the course of the celebration, they competed against one another in a softball series. The losing team had to clean the house of the winner. Nick's team lost.

As he reported for the cleaning detail, he was handed a dust rag and told to polish everything that didn't move. As he worked, he kept his eyes open, and when the kid from New York turned his back, Nick very quietly slipped out the back door. Gretchen was living just three blocks away and he couldn't resist the temptation to see her. She was undergoing outpatient group therapy offered by the Fort Lauderdale *Spectrum,* so she was aware of what was happening with Nick, but she didn't dream he'd be able to visit her. When she saw him coming down the driveway toward the house, she whooped with joy and ran to meet him.

"Nick, darling," she cried as he swept her up in his arms, "how long can you sta..."

He stopped her question with a kiss, picked her up and carried her back into the apartment. "I may not have very long, so let's not waste time."

"Do they know you're here?" she asked.

"No," he answered, laughing softly, "I just took off when nobody was looking."

"Nick," Gretchen cautioned, "you're violating your probation. If you're caught, they can cancel all the time you've put in and make you start over. They might even cancel your probation and send you to prison. Are you sure this is what you want to do?"

He didn't answer that question until six hours later. For a little while, their entire world was composed of just the two of them, but after smoking a couple of joints, Nick began to pull his thoughts together. Gretchen was right. He was on the downhill side of the *Spectrum* program and he'd be some kind of fool to give up so close to the end.

"Look, honey," he murmured, "I've got to go back. They'll probably make me do something silly and stupid for leaving, but if I go in without them coming after me, I may get off easy."

Gretchen agreed, saying, "I don't want you to go, but I don't want you to get caught either. You know I love you and that I'll be here when you get out, so take off, darling, and be careful."

Returning to the house, Nick was amazed to find the cleaning crew still working. He slipped in the back door and found his dust rag right where he'd left it six hours earlier. Picking it up, he took a couple of swipes at the woodwork in the hallway and then sauntered into the dining room. Nobody said a word to him; even the kid from New York was smiling his approval of the work that had been done.

They don't know I've been gone, Nick realized. *They all think I've been here the full time.* He felt like laughing and telling everyone how he'd fooled them, but smiling to himself, he remained silent. He'd seen Gretchen, smoked a little dope and had a wonderful time, so why brag. *Besides,* he thought, *if they ever do this again, I might want to pull a repeat*

52

performance, and if they know about it, they'll be on the alert.

Nick wasn't a letter writer, so Gretchen had no way of knowing how he'd fared. She wondered about it for several weeks before an opportunity came up for her to learn what happened. One evening, while she and her friend, Kathy, were attending their outpatient therapy group meeting, the kid from New York was introduced as a guest leader. He told them about the *Spectrum* inpatient program and how the Miami house operated. Gretchen figured he might know Nick, so after the session, she asked him what had happened to Nick when he returned to the housecleaning.

"I don't understand your question," the kid told her. "If you can tell me a little more about the event, maybe I can give you an answer."

Gretchen explained that Nick had paid her a visit, giving him all the details about Nick's decision to return to the program. She was proud of how he had accepted the responsibility of returning and told the kid that she thought Nick was really getting a lot out of the program.

Never letting Gretchen know why he wanted all the details, the kid pumped her for the whole story. She didn't tell him about the dope, but she did reveal that Nick had spent six hours with her. The kid gave her the impression that Nick had done nothing that wasn't permitted, and he promised to tell Nick that he'd had a nice visit with her.

"I'll let him know how much you enjoyed seeing him," the kid told Gretchen, "and I know Nick will be pleased to learn that we talked."

"Give him my love," Gretchen urged, "and tell him that I'm still waiting for his release from the program."

"Oh I will," the kid promised, turning to leave.

"Thank you," Gretchen responded, thinking what

a nice guy he seemed to be.

The next morning, Nick was called into the office for a conference with the assistant director. As he entered, the smile on the kid's face told him something was about to happen. After being told to sit down, he waited for the kid to finish reading from a file folder and wondered what he could have done to make the kid seem so happy.

"You know, Nick," the kid said, still looking at the file, "that's a cute little dolly you got." Looking up, he continued, "She's much too young for a guy your age and there's probably some sex charges that could be brought against you, but she sure is a sweet little thing."

Down deep in the pit of his stomach, Nick began to feel his emotions coming to a boil.

"Gretchen and I had a nice little visit last night," the kid smirked. "She told me a lot of interesting things about you."

"What kind of things?" Nick asked.

"Oh we'll get to that," the kid answered, "but first I want to know what you did that day when we were all together at the house in Fort Lauderdale. It seems that you were quite active that day. Tell me, just what did you do?"

Knowing there was no sense in lying about what had happened, or even trying to face an alibi, Nick said, "While everybody was cleaning that house, I took off and spent the afternoon with my girl."

"How long were you gone?"

"About five or six hours," Nick stated flatly.

"Did you have sex with her?"

Nick refused to answer. He caught the kid's eyes and gave him a cold stare.

"Did you shoot dope before going to bed with her, or afterwards?"

Nick remained silent.

"Come on, man," the kid insisted, "she's too cute

54

to pass up. You might as well admit everything."

"I went to see her and that's all you need to know," Nick stated firmly.

"Did you bring any dope back with you?" the kid pressed.

Nick shook his head.

"Did your little dolly give you any money?"

Silence was all the answer he got.

"Have you hooked her on drugs and turned her out?"

The anger in Nick's stomach was no longer simmering. It was boiling.

"I know all about that afternoon," the kid bragged.

"What are you going to do about it?" Nick demanded.

"I'm going to have you sit out in the hallway and cool your heels while I decide on your punishment," the kid snapped. "Now, get out of here and wait. I'll call you back in when I'm ready to settle your hash." He grinned malevolently before adding, "I could send you to prison, you know."

While Nick sat in the hallway and waited, his anger seemed to change. He knew the kid was trying to push his buttons again, so he slowly forced himself to calm down. *I'm older and smarter than that little punk,* he silently told himself. *I'll have to go along with whatever he decides, right now, but this program is for the birds and I'm getting out of here as soon as possible.* After about an hour's wait, the kid opened the door to his office and told Nick to come in and take his medicine. He didn't ask him to sit down this time.

"Okay, Nick," he declared contemptuously, "I'm going to take it easy on you this time, but if you get out of line just one more time, I'll fix you up with some hard-time behind bars." He couldn't help grinning with smug satisfaction as he added, "All I want this time is your hair!"

55

Expecting worse, Nick thought, *At least I won't have to parade around in diapers or wearing a sign. He can have my hair, but that isn't going to be the end of it by a long shot.* Capturing the kid's eyes with his, Nick said, "Okay, take my hair, but as soon as it grows out enough to make me look human again, I'll be gone."

Shaking his head, the kid laughed. "No way, Nickie baby. You're not leaving the program until I'm good and ready to let you go. Now, run along to the barber like a good boy," he hardened his voice, "and get your head shaved!" He laughed a little harder before he snarled, "After it's done, I want you back here for inspection. Understand?"

"Yes, sir," Nick barked, giving the kid a stiff-finger salute as he turned and left the office.

In addition to losing his hair, Nick was given a work contract which required him to dust and polish a spotless room from 6:00 a.m. until midnight every day. He wasn't allowed to talk to anyone and had to eat by himself. While his hair was growing out, he put up with the foolishness and didn't complain, but after two months, he made the decision to leave the program.

This was not difficult to do. Everyone was accustomed to his being by himself, so from his isolation he just walked out of the house and thumbed a ride on U. S. Highway 1 leading out of Miami for Ft. Lauderdale where he knew Gretchen would be waiting. Nick knew the kid would report him missing, so he decided to see both his probation officer and the judge on the following day. He felt certain he could run another game on them and get completely out of the *Spectrum* program.

As planned, Nick appeared before the judge voluntarily and pleaded, "Your Honor, I realize that I have a serious drug problem and that I need help to overcome it, but *Spectrum House* isn't the kind of help I need."

"How so?" the judge inquired.

"The *Spectrum* program," Nick explained, "is based mainly on intimidation and humiliation. They put grown men in diapers and treat them like babies. I've had my head shaved and been required to do useless work. This was done as punishment without regard for my drug addiction or my rehabilitation. It had nothing to do with my drug habit and was applied by the house's assistant director just to humiliate me and demonstrate his power to punish me."

"What do you suggest we do with you?" the judge asked.

"Your Honor," Nick replied, "I'm more than willing to submit to a schedule of urine tests and group therapy on a regular basis on the outside. At least then," he added, "I could get help from a knowledgeable counselor and relate what I learned to my immediate problem without having to tolerate a lot of silly, childish and stupid egotistical nonsense."

The judge conferred briefly with Nick's probation officer and then ruled in Nick's favor. He was allowed to join Gretchen's group therapy sessions and excused from the *Spectrum Program*. He scored some heroin on the way back to the apartment and went straight into the bathroom for a fix before telling Gretchen the good news.

She was aware of what he was doing. Her friend, Kathy had tipped her off to his heroin addiction. As she waited for him to come out and face her, she resolved to try heroin herself. She wanted the same satisfaction and peace he seemed to get from the drug. She also wanted to be on his wave length in everything he did. *If he's going to be on the needle,* she silently decided, *then so am I.*

57

Gretchen is just skin and bones from heroin addiction

Gretchen and Nick after Spectrum House Program

GETTING IT ON
WITH HEROIN

"Whipping and abuse are like narcotics: you have to double the dose as the sensibilities decline."

Harriet Beecher Stowe
(1811 - 1896)

With Nick back, Gretchen was much happier. She had missed him terribly, but she knew he was using heroin and she felt cheated because he refused to share it with her. He wasn't the same Nick. She began to resent the feeling that she was living with two different Nicks—a short-tempered one before the bathroom fix and a mellow one after it. She decided it was time for her to enjoy the treat with him. They'd been together for a year, and she was certain they'd be together for the rest of their lives, so whatever he did, she wanted to share.

As he came out of the bathroom at their apartment, she asked, "What are you using?"

"Just something I picked up," he answered. "It's nothing you'd be interested in."

"Hey," she insisted, "you're using heroin and I want some, too."

"Let's drop it, Gretchen," he growled.

"No way," she yelled. "If it's good enough for you, it's good enough for me. You're getting much more out of it than I ever get from my reefer or speed."

"You don't want this," he snapped, "and I'm not going to let you have it!"

That wasn't the answer Gretchen wanted, but she

could see his anger building, so she didn't press the matter. She had no intention of giving up, but for the moment she let it slide.

A couple of days later, she brought it up again. He seemed in a better mood so she went for it. "You're doing heroin and I want you to get me off as well."

"No you don't," he declared flatly. "Heroin isn't something I ever want you fooling around with."

"It sure works for you," she countered. "It seems to give you peace, and that's what I want."

"You're too young," he argued, "and girls can't handle heroin the same as a man. Every girl I know who's using it is on the street, hooking for the guy who turned her on to it. That's not a life I want for you."

Again, Gretchen didn't push. She knew Nick was right, but she still wanted to experience the results he seemed to be getting. As the weeks passed and Nick got further and further into the business, his need for more and more heroin became evident to Gretchen, but she still didn't foresee what might happen to her if she started using it. As she began spending more time with him on his buying and selling trips, their arguments increased in frequency and intensity.

The more they fought and argued about it, the more desperate Gretchen became. She began to question the value of her life. She felt she was losing her mind. Most of this depression was a result of the speed she was using, but that didn't register in her thinking. Nick wouldn't talk about it, so she turned to her friend, Kathy, for sympathy and comfort. Nick was off peddling dope and the two girls were alone in the apartment.

"Kathy," Gretchen said, "my life isn't making any sense. I simply don't know why I'm alive. Nothing seems to count anymore and I can't even see meaning in anyone else's life."

"I know what you mean," Kathy agreed.

"Yeh," Gretchen continued, "but Nick's not bothered by any of these things. He goes in the bathroom every morning looking like a grumpy mess, and when he comes out he's all smiles, on top of the world."

"He's shooting up," Kathy agreed. "Several months ago, he asked me to buy him the cosmetics he needed to cover the tracks on his arms."

"Well, when he comes home this afternoon," Gretchen stated firmly, "He's going to get me off or it's over between us! It's gotten to the point where I can't even talk to him anymore. He won't discuss heroin with me and he still hasn't actually admitted using it."

"Take it easy, honey," Kathy advised. "He's an addict and he knows what heroin can do. He's only trying to protect you and keep the *monkey* off your back."

"I don't care," Gretchen replied. "I can't go on like this any longer. Nick and I are partners and he's either going to accept me as such in everything he does, or I'm walking."

Kathy left about an hour before Nick returned. Gretchen used that time to sharpen her feminine wiles. She knew how to turn him on and reduce him to putty in her hands. She was a beautiful young woman and she intended to use her charms to win this struggle with him.

After a shower, she dried and brushed her hair into the style she knew he liked best, did her nails his favorite color and matched them with her lipstick. Tiny gold earrings reflected the sparkle in her eyes and smile. She added a gold chain to accent her long, slender neck. Slipping into the lovely, pale yellow dress he always complimented her on, she added a pair of soft leather pumps. After checking herself in the mirror, she walked into the living room and gracefully settled into the wing chair near the

61

window. It was just beginning to get dark when the headlights of Nick's car swung into the driveway.

Gretchen knew she looked lovely and desirable. Her makeup was flawless, her perfume was Nick's favorite. The soft evening air held the scent with a delicate caress. Her plan was set. Nick would either agree to give her the heroin she wanted, making her a full partner in his life, or their relationship would come to a screeching halt. She held her breath as she heard him slam the car door and head for the apartment.

Nick burst through the front door. He looked neither right nor left, but charged straight through to the bathroom. He hadn't even glanced at her. He was in there shooting up. He wanted his heroin-high more than he wanted her. Her resolution to win grew stronger.

Waiting quietly, Gretchen didn't move from the chair. She knew he would be in a better mood when he came out of the bathroom. His need would be pacified and his interest would be back on her. As he opened the bathroom door, the mirror reflected a soft glowing light directly at Gretchen. Nick didn't miss seeing her this time. She could almost feel the warmth streaming from his eyes as they swept over her from the tips of her toes to the gleaming crest of her hair.

Her voice was low, soft and controlled as she spoke. "Nick, I want the same thing you just gave yourself in the bathroom."

"No," he groaned, moving toward her.

"Yes," she demanded. "It's either that, or I'm going to go out and find someone who will give it to me. You'll either share your heroin with me, or I'll no longer share myself with you."

"Why?" he asked.

"I want what you've got," she answered. "Your life has meaning; mine's worth nothing. You seem to get

62

peace from heroin while I'm tormented by things I can't understand. I love you, Nick, but if you keep shutting me out of what you're doing, that love will not survive." She stood up and stepped toward him. "Please, darling, get me off and let me feel what you're feeling. Please let me back into your life."

She wanted to rush into his arms. She wanted to feel the strength he could give her, but she stood stone-still and waited for him to react to her demand.

Nick's mind filled with pictures of Gretchen with someone else, Gretchen turned out on the street, Gretchen hooking for her supplier.

"Okay," he agreed, after a long pause, "but you won't like it and I want you to know that I don't like giving it to you."

"Darling," she sighed, "I know I'll like it."

Shaking his head, Nick reluctantly turned back toward the bathroom. When he returned, the needle was ready. Smiling at him with love and gratitude, Gretchen watched as he tied his belt around her slender arm just above the elbow. Making certain there was no air in the syringe, Nick found the vein he needed. Gretchen watched as he brought the needle down to her arm. She closed her eyes as she felt the needle break the skin. She wasn't sure what to expect from the shot, but what she got was nothing like what she wanted.

As the heroin entered her bloodstream her entire body wound up into a series of tight little balls. Gretchen's stomach twisted inside her and every breath she took was labored. She was seized by the fear that she was dying. There was no escape from this feeling. Its impact was overwhelming. Her stomach turned again and she wanted to throw up. Tears of pain and confusion were streaming down her cheeks. Gretchen's mind turned on her as she screamed in desperation and despair. Nick's concerned face was just a blur in her eyes. Death seemed

63

her only way out. She didn't want this terrible feeling to go on, and suddenly she was afraid she wouldn't die and the feeling would never end.

Gretchen was no longer concerned with her great questions about the purpose of life. It didn't seem to matter any longer. She slowly became aware of a growing peace about living and dying. Her brain was gathering the protective armor of mental indifference about it. The feeling of discomfort was fading, but the memory of her initial reaction was fresh in her mind.

For the next 24 hours, Gretchen pondered the effect she'd felt from the shot. At first she didn't want any more to do with heroin, but as the day wore on, her thoughts and desires changed. The drug hadn't provided answers to any of the questions troubling her, but her pressing need for those answers was gone. Heroin had given her a way to cope with them and she concluded nothing else held the answers to her questions.

Later that afternoon, she stuck her arm out to Nick again. This time none of the unpleasantness occurred. She felt entirely engulfed in a warm, peaceful cocoon. *This is what I've been looking for all my life,* she thought. *I don't need answers now. I've got a warm glow in my heart and the mystery of life has vanished.* Gretchen was hooked. She was convinced heroin was the answer. She and Nick were sharing everything, and nothing else mattered to her. All her problems were still there, none had gone away, but she no longer cared.

LOVING BRUTALITY

"O'er waiting harp-strings of the mind
There sweeps a strain,
Low, sad, and sweet, whose measures bind
The power of pain."

Mary Baker Eddy
(1821 - 1910)

As his addiction to heroin grew, Nick enhanced the enjoyment it gave him by inflicting pain on others. This facet of his personality also attracted Gretchen. Her submissive soul needed his physical domination. If she did something he didn't like, or disputed something he was doing, he would often slap her around. Gretchen knew there was a line in their relationship that she shouldn't cross, but she often crossed it just to test him. Although she didn't enjoy the physical pain, she wanted to know he cared enough about her to inflict it.

Nick loved physical violence. He relished danger both for the fear it created in him and the challenge it gave him. Even before the near-killing at the *Four O'Clock Club*, Nick relished the rush he obtained from dominating other people. He loved the feeling of power. This was demonstrated by the pride he took in controlling the actions of his listeners when he played suggestive music over the radio.

Even though he'd refused to inject Gretchen for so many months, there was a limited degree of personal satisfaction for him when she insisted on joining him in his addiction. Without admitting it to himself, he secretly took pride in the fact that she loved him so much she wanted to emulate his use of heroin. Her addiction added to the demands he now faced on a daily basis, the problem of supplying enough heroin for two growing habits. This forced him to expand his dealing and improve his ongoing relationship with his primary source of supply.

In some ways, his use of heroin was related to his need for excitement. It contained an element of fear, the fear of addiction, which he enjoyed overcoming by sticking a needle in his arm. Heroin had the power to change that fear into pleasure, and the pleasure led Nick into doing things that created a greater fear for him to conquer with violence and brutality. He only felt complete as a man when he was confronted by a fear that he could overcome. He was only happy when he could risk everything and win by using his nerve, strength, and cunning to achieve his desired objective. Nick accepted his probation as a challenge and acted accordingly.

When Nick met with his probation officer for the first time after being released from the *Spectrum* program, he was faced with a situation he couldn't ignore. The man obviously believed that Nick belonged in prison and made no attempt to conceal his feelings.

"Mr. Barbetta," he declared openly, "I know you're involved in the sale of illegal drugs. You belong behind bars and I intend to catch you in violation of your probation and get you off the streets."

Smiling confidently, Nick replied, "You've got me all wrong. I've changed. I'm into the counseling program, and all that other stuff is behind me."

"I don't think so," the officer countered. "You're a junkie and I want you to know that I'm going to watch you like a hawk."

"That's okay by me," Nick said, "but I'm not

going to give you any trouble, so every minute you spend watching me will just be a waste of your time."

A few days later, Nick and Gretchen were shopping in a downtown department store when they spotted the probation officer following them. When they stopped to look at something, the man would slip behind a pillar or a display, remaining out of sight until they moved on to another counter.

"Doesn't he have anything else to do?" Gretchen whispered.

"I know I'm not the only guy on his case book," Nick answered. "You'd think he couldn't spend all this time following me."

This type of surveillance served as a warning to Nick. The only thing the man could learn by following them on a shopping tour was how much money they were spending. Nick wasn't working at a regular job, so if he spent a large amount of money, the officer could ask how he got it. This could lead to other embarrassing questions. Money was rolling in from Nick's heroin dealings, but he could hardly claim that as a legitimate source of income. They left the store without making any purchase.

"We've got to be careful," Nick explained to Gretchen as they walked to the car. "If we flash too much money around, he'll come down on me with even greater surveillance."

"He's getting to be a real pest," Gretchen grumbled. "Next thing you know, he'll be coming to the apartment to see if we're sleeping together."

Gretchen had touched on another of Nick's probation problems. The officer didn't like the idea of him sleeping with a minor. The fact that if they were living together it was with her mother's apparent approval didn't influence the man's thinking at all. Gretchen was 16 years old and Nick was 27. Since Nick wasn't supposed to be living with Gretchen, they tried to hide their living arrangement, and Nick kept most of his clothes at a friend's. The officer suspected as much and wanted to catch them in the act, but for some reason, perhaps his case load was too heavy, he didn't follow up on his suspicions. That came later when a new probation officer was assigned to Nick's case.

When the first officer moved on to the Federal Probation Agency, he briefed his replacement on the status of Nick's behavior. The new man was a churchgoing Christian, so the relationship between Gretchen and Nick took on more importance with him. Nick thought the P.O. would be easy to fool, and in many ways he was, but it didn't take long for him to display his suspicions about their living together.

There are rules and regulations that govern the conduct of all probation officers, but this doesn't prevent them from using the law to further their personal feelings when these feelings are within the law. A matter of morality can be enforced, or overlooked by the officer, according to the importance he feels it holds in the rehabilitation of the man on probation. In Nick's case, the new man held strong feelings about young girls living with older men without benefit of marriage.

The smart thing for Nick would have been to move out and forget about Gretchen, but the love they shared was too great for that. He couldn't think of life without her and she didn't want to live without him. For most people this would have been a challenge they couldn't meet, but like Bonnie and Clyde before them, they were bound together in the life they were leading by their mutual desires and the challenge itself.

Knowing the attitude of the probation officer, they made every effort to give the appearance of living separately. Nick's few clothes were not kept in the apartment closet next to hers. A casual visitor would have been unable to discern that they were living together. He didn't leave his shaving kit in the bathroom. They never left their dinner dishes out on the table where it would have been obvious that they'd shared a meal. Most importantly of all, there was never a trace of Nick's drug traffic left about where it could be discovered and related to Gretchen. By doing all of this, they were successful in deceiving the probation officer as to the true nature of their relationship. He tried to catch them, but failed.

Probation officers do not have to give warning before making a visit, so it came as no surprise when he showed up one evening at a little past 11:00 o'clock. They knew he would come eventually and when he knocked on the apartment door, Gretchen answered.

"Can I help you?" she asked.

"I'm Roger Thornton, Nick Barbetta's probation officer," he replied. "Is Nick around?"

"Yes," she admitted. "He was just getting ready to leave, but if you'd like to see him, please come in."

Stepping through the doorway, he asked, "Doesn't Mr. Barbetta live here with you?"

"Oh no," she lied, "this is just his mailing address. We're still friends and he comes by quite often to pick up the mail, but he doesn't live here."

Coming out of the kitchen, Nick smiled and greeted the officer. "Hi, Roger. I was just leaving. What can I do for you?"

They made a point of never smart-mouthing a probation officer. Nick had heard other men tell stories of how they insulted people in authority and he knew what they got in return for their remarks. With this in mind, Gretchen volunteered to make a fresh pot of coffee and invited Roger to stay for a cup.

"No, thanks," Roger responded. "It's getting late, so I'll just go along with Nick." Giving her a friendly nod, he added, "I just wanted to make sure he wasn't violating his probation by forcing himself on you."

"We're friends," Gretchen assured him as they walked to the door, "but Nick has learned his lesson and wouldn't do anything to violate his probation."

"I'm glad to hear that," Roger said. "He still has several months to go before it ends and a mistake now could be very foolish."

The two men spoke briefly before getting into their cars and driving away. Nick followed Roger's car to the corner, where the probation office turned right while Nick drove straight ahead. As far as Roger knew, Nick was still living with a friend on the other side of town. He'd seen Nick's clothes there and the man had confirmed that Nick was living with him until he found a place of his own.

After driving around for a few minutes, Nick turned back toward the apartment. He cruised by to be certain that Roger's car wasn't parked in the dark waiting his return. When the coast was clear, he pulled into the driveway. Gretchen was waiting in the darkened living room and she laughed softly as he entered the apartment.

"I think Roger gets his kicks by spying on us," she chuckled.

"Yeh," Nick agreed, "he's a frustrated peeping-Tom."

"He knows we're both in group therapy," she griped, "so why can't he leave us alone?"

"It's his thing," Nick muttered, heading for the bedroom. "Come on, it's late and we need our sleep. We fooled the little pervert this time, but we've still got to be extra careful with his snooping around all the time."

Joining him in the bedroom, Gretchen said, "Oh yeah, that guy, Tony, the man Rick told you about, he phoned while you were out. He's got some stuff he wants you to try. He's going to have Rick bring it around, and if you like it, he can supply it on a regular basis."

70

"Did he say anything else?"

"Only that this is some primo stuff that just arrived from Central America."

"When's Rick supposed to bring it over?"

"Tomorrow night," Gretchen answered.

Chuckling, Nick observed, "Good thing he didn't come tonight. Roger would've had a ball with us if we'd been high when he showed up for his surprise visit."

"Yeah," Gretchen agreed with a grin, "it's also a good thing that we'd planned on watching the 'Tonight' show. If he'd caught us in bed asleep like most of his friends probably are at 11:00 every night, it would have been too bad."

Rick's friendship with Nick went back to their "hippie" days when they both felt they were pioneers on the drug frontier. It was Rick who got him started dealing heroin and if he felt he was onto something good from south of the border, it was probably going to be stuff of top quality. This interested Nick because his business was growing and he wanted some stuff that he could cut a few more times without losing too much of the kick. Every cut he made meant that much more profit on the deal, so a reliable source of quality merchandise would be very valuable.

As a new addict, Gretchen's need for heroin wasn't so demanding and overwhelming. She was a *special occasion* user and most of her needs were met on weekends. Nick, however, was far beyond that. He needed a daily fix and the cost of his habit continued to grow. It jumped from a few hundred dollars a week to well over $700 per day. This was no *monkey* on his back, it was a full-grown *ape*. As a dealer, he could handle the increase. $4,900 per week was just a small percentage of his incoming take, and if the sample Rick was bringing over proved to be *pure,* there'd be no end to the money he could make. As it was, he and Gretchen were hard-pressed to find places to hide their cash and she would groan with boredom when he showed up with another bag full of $100 bills. Regardless of this, they eagerly awaited Rick's arrival the following evening.

Sitting around the kitchen table, Rick, Gretchen and Nick faced each other over glasses of chilled chablis. They were good friends, about to share something new and exciting. As Rick laid his sample out on the table and slowly unfolded its waxed paper container, there was a note of professional pride in his voice.

"This is the purest of the pure," he bragged. "It can be cut six or seven times before taking it to the street for another four or five cuttings." Pushing it across the table toward Nick, he smiled, "Try a touch and see if it isn't what I'm saying, but take it easy because you've never had anything this good before."

Nick fixed a spoon for himself and Gretchen, making it lighter in both cases than either of them usually took. After getting off, he let the sensation sweep over him as he administered the needle to Gretchen. It was glorious and he said as much.

"I've never had anything like this in my life," he crowed. "It's the ultimate! It's the perfect *pure*." Looking at Gretchen, he expected her to confirm his evaluation of the drug, but she was out of it. Her face was vacant as she slowly got to her feet and floated toward the bedroom.

"I feel, I feel..." she stammered in a slurred voice, not finishing what she started to say.

The two men watched her turn on the bedroom television and sit on the edge of the bed. She seemed to be pretty loaded, but she was watching the Perry Mason show, so they went back to talking business.

A few minutes later, when Nick glanced back into the bedroom, Gretchen had slipped from the bed to the floor. Somewhere in the back of his mind the overdose flag began flying at the top of his mental flagpole. With Rick's help, he got her on her feet and started walking her back to reality. When she finally started making sense again, she confirmed the purity of the Central American heroin.

"Ooooh," she sighed, "that stuff's great. I was watching Perry Mason, and suddenly his voice got very loud and that's the last thing I can remember." Putting her head on Nick's shoulder, she added, "That is until you were telling me to keep walking and wake up. Thank you, lover, for bringing me back."

"Gretchen," Nick exclaimed with relief, "you overdosed. You could have died!"

"I know," she admitted. "I've never felt so hopeless and helpless in my life. I can't remember what happened, but I was alone in a black, dark place. Oh, Nick, it was horrible!" Locking her eyes on his, she demanded, "Don't ever let me do that again!"

"Don't worry, honey," he assured her, "now that we know what this stuff is and what it can do, we'll keep it under control." That was an impossibility for a junkie, and down deep in his heart Nick knew it, but at the time, he still believed they were in control of the heroin they were using.

The deal between Rick and Nick was struck. It opened the floodgates to unbelievable profits. Every drawer in the apartment was rapidly filled with money. It got to the point where they didn't even bother to count it, they just shoved it in to get it out of sight.

As the months passed, Nick's probation surveillance faded away to nothing. He still had time to serve, but no one seemed overly interested in his activities. He hadn't done anything to attract attention to himself and that's the way he intended to keep it. The management of the radio station also wanted him back on the air. His notoriety had faded, so going back to the all-night D.J. routine gave him the perfect cover for his drug dealing.

Nick's listening audience, where he had the greatest following, was among the *night-people*. They were bartenders, hookers, cab drivers, gas station attendants, high-rollers and fun seekers. They were the folks who knew what he was into and agreed with his eat, drink, shoot-up, you-only-live-once philosophy. They were the swingers, party-goers and those who lived in the *fast lane* of life. Nick still had a faithful following among the teens during the early part of every night's shift, so he could put out the music he wanted them to hear and keep them on his hip. In a very big way, he was in the perfect position to promote the ongoing use of drugs by his *night-people* and to influence the attitudes of his younger listeners. Returning to the station also made it possible for him to spend some of the money they were taking in because he had a viable, visible job.

Gretchen started wearing real diamonds and pearls. She was able to buy expensive designer clothes. They ate all their meals in the best, most expensive restaurants. Nick always had the best seats wherever they went—rock concerts or Muhammed Ali fights. He drove Lincoln Continentals loaded with every conceivable extra option. All this was part of his image that conveyed the good life to his listeners and fans. To the subculture and the night-life underground, Nick was fast becoming a minor legend and role-model. He spent money grandly, always leaving big tips for bartenders and waitresses, but he never wrote a check. Everything was paid for in cash. There was no record of his wealth and he was careful in his lifestyle to impress only those he wanted to impress.

It took Nick a little over a year to become the primary source for heroin in south Florida. Over seventy percent of all the "H" consumed in Miami, Fort Lauderdale, Hollywood and the surrounding towns and suburbs was passing through his hands. He and Gretchen were riding high on a wave of big money, crime and political corruption.

If he were arrested, which happened several times, he was never sent to prison. Nick did short periods of county time and probation, but he was never handed any serious *hard-time* that would keep him out of circulation for more than four or five months. None of this slowed him down or changed his lifestyle in any way. While he was gone, Gretchen had enough dope to keep her from hurting until he returned.

One afternoon in 1973, Nick and a friend were killing time in Miami, waiting for a drug deal to come down, when Nick decided he needed a motorcycle. He'd seen a couple of people riding bikes on their way into the city and the idea of having one for himself was suddenly appealing.

They were having a couple of beers when he said, "Albert, let's wander over to the Harley-Davidson dealer and do some shopping."

"Okay," Albert agreed, "but don't get the bright idea of trying to get me on one of those crazy machines. When I travel, I like comfort and air conditioning. I've seen too many bikers with bugs stuck on their teeth, and having the wind in my hair ain't my idea of having a good time."

Walking into the showroom, Nick looked over all the models on display and picked the most expensive, a Harley-Davidson sportster. He climbed on the saddle and liked the way it felt. It was a big, solid machine and the weight of it gave him a sense of power. He was grinning like a kid with a new toy when the salesman approached.

"That's a great bike," the man said.

"I like it," Nick responded with enthusiasm. "Can I take this one out for a ride?"

"Have you ridden bikes before?"

"Sure," Nick answered.

"Then take her out," the salesman said with a friendly smile.

Nick was gone about ten minutes. He rode it around the block a couple of times before wheeling it back to the showroom. Albert and the salesman both grinned as he parked the bike but remained in the saddle.

"How much for this one?" Nick asked.

"That's our finest model," the man informed him.

"Yeah," Nick said, "but how much do you want for it?"

"She's ready to go, all serviced and everything," the man added.

"How much money do you want for it?" Nick repeated.

"The price, including tax and license, is $3,795."

"Done," Nick roared, reaching in his pocket. Pulling out a roll of $100 bills, he peeled off 38 of them and handed the wad to the salesman. "I want you to buy yourself a beer with the change," he chortled. "Make out the papers. You just sold your most expensive bike."

"Yes, sir!" the salesman exclaimed. "It'll take just a minute to do the paperwork." Handing Nick a booklet, he added, "Here's your owner's manual. You might like to glance through it while you're waiting."

Turning to Albert, Nick laughed. "Here, you read it. As long as the thing runs, I'll ride it. When it stops running, I'll junk it and buy me another one."

"I don't wanna read it," Albert grumbled. "It ain't my bike."

"Then throw it away," Nick instructed. "I'll never need it." Grinning with pleasure, he added, "After we finish our business here in town, you can drive my car back and I'll ride my bike. Gretchen is going to love

76

this thing and if she does, I'll come back and get one for her. How do you think I look on one of these?"

Laughing softly, Albert replied, "Like you've got more money than brains. Those things are dangerous. You can kill yourself without half trying."

"I know," Nick agreed, more to himself than to his friend, "that's why I got it. I like what danger does to me. It turns me on and having all this power between my legs makes the danger even more personal and meaningful."

Nick—"I like what danger does to me."

**Nick—The walking dead—
$700 a day drug habit**

DEATH IS A SILENT VISITOR

"The Angel of Death has been abroad throughout the land: you may almost hear the beating of his wings."

John Bright
(1811 - 1889)

Gretchen and Nick spent most of the day cutting the heroin he brought back from Miami. While working, they discussed the idea of moving away from her mother's and getting a place of their own. The memory of Madeleine calling the cops while they were cutting dope was still fresh in their minds. Since they could easily afford a bigger and better place, the decision was made.

Gretchen began looking through the afternoon paper, reading the rental ads, while Nick put their day's work out of sight. As she found a couple of likely places and was making phone calls to set up early appointments, John, a long-time friend of Nick's, stopped by for a visit. The two men talked and drank a few beers in the kitchen.

"Nick," John said, "it's been quite a while since I last saw you. Are you still in the business?"

Nick nodded.

"Well, I've broken away," John revealed with an uncertain smile. "I've been clean for over three months."

As he went on, telling about how he'd fought his addiction and finally felt free again, Nick wondered why he'd come by. *If he's clean,* Nick silently questioned, *why in the world does he want to know*

79

if I'm still dealing? Could he be working with the cops, trying to set me up to beat a rap they've nailed him with, or is he just curious?

"I'm as clean as the Board of Health," John continued, "and I can't tell you how much better I've been feeling. I'm ready to go back to work and make an honest living again."

"*Here it comes,* Nick thought, *he needs some money to tide him over until he can get back on his feet. I'll wait until he asks for it and then I'll give him whatever he needs.*" Just as Nick was about to ask if there was anything he could do to help his old friend, Gretchen came out of the living room with a big smile on her lovely face.

"There's a place in Hollywood that sounds just great," she announced happily, "but it won't last long and the agent is willing to show it to us right now if we want to see it."

"Sounds okay to me," Nick replied, looking at John. "Would you like to come with us?"

"Naw," he said, "I'm a little tired, but if you don't mind, I'd like to wait here for you guys to come back. If you decide to take this new place, maybe I can help you move."

"John, you're more than welcome to stay and rest," Gretchen said. "In fact, if you want to lie down and take a little nap, help yourself. When we get back, we'll all go out to dinner and have a nice visit." She opened the bedroom door and pointed to the bed. "Just make yourself at home, and if this place is what we're looking for, we'll take you up on your offer to help."

"Yeah," Nick agreed, thinking he knew of a way to give his friend some money without it seeming like charity, "we'll even make it worth your while. Do you still have a driver's license?"

"Sure do," John answered.

"Good," Nick said, getting up from the table.

"We'll rent a truck and you can be our mover."

"We'll be back in a couple of hours," Gretchen added, "and if you get thirsty, there's beer in the fridge. Help yourself."

During the drive to Hollywood, Gretchen gave Nick the address of the new apartment before she asked, "Do you really think John has kicked his habit?"

"Yeah," he replied, "but I think he needs money to keep body and soul together until he gets back on his feet." Taking his eyes off the road for a moment, he glanced at Gretchen and smiled. "Having him help us move will make it easy for us to give him the money he needs without making him beg for help."

"I wonder," Gretchen murmured, "if that's really why he came to see us. He didn't take off his jacket, and with only a tee shirt under it, maybe he didn't want us to see fresh tracks on his arms. He knows we're still in the business and I think he came over for a fix."

"Naw," Nick said, "I'm sure he's clean. If he wasn't he'd have asked for a set-up to get back in the business. He knows I'd trust him with enough dope to get started again."

"You're probably right," Gretchen concluded as they stopped in front of the new apartment building. "In any event, we'll get the whole story when we take him to dinner."

It was still early in the afternoon when they returned. Gretchen was excited about the new place and Nick was pleased with the lease they'd signed. They agreed to rent the truck and get John started on the move as they got out of the car and went inside.

John was lying on the kitchen floor. The hypodermic needle was still stuck in his arm. He was comatose from an accidental overdose. Nick tried to get him up on his feet, but he was like a limp rag doll. They worked on him for over three hours before calling Rick for help. Gretchen was exhausted and Nick's strength was fading fast.

When Rick arrived, he took over to give Nick a little rest. John's breathing was very shallow and every time they relaxed the least bit, he started turning blue. They repeatedly worked on him and got his blood flowing again, but the moment they eased up, he faded out on them. Rick suggested putting him on the bed and commented, "I think he's going to be okay. He's just having a really heavy high."

Another half hour passed with no change in John. At least he wasn't getting worse, which gave them hope that Rick was right. As he left, Rick added, "His blood seems to be flowing on its own now, so just let him sleep it off. Where'd he get the stuff?

"He must have brought it with him," Nick answered. "None of my stuff has been touched."

"There's some new dope on the street," Rick said. "It's deadly. A lot of people are going out on it. He must have scored some of that and come over to your place to crash. When he comes around, find out what he's into."

As they watched Rick back his car out to the street, Gretchen took a deep breath and sighed, "I'm wringing wet. I've got to take a shower and get into some fresh clothes."

"Me, too," Nick agreed. "I never realized how big and heavy John had become. Lugging him around is a real workout."

John was still unconscious, but breathing, as they undressed in the bedroom and got their change of clothes. Nick checked him again before joining Gretchen in the shower. The cool water refreshed them, and when they were once again dressed, she went to the bedroom for her makeup.

"Nick, get in here!" she yelled. "John isn't breathing!"

They both worked up another sweat trying to

revive him. They did everything they could think of, but John was dead. Having come so close to death herself from an overdose, Gretchen took it very hard. Every time she looked at John, she saw herself lying there and the finality of death hit with a powerful impact. She suddenly knew that Death was a silent visitor. He came without a sound, and having arrived, he rarely left empty-handed.

Nick's thoughts ran in a more practical vein. He knew the police would have to be called. He considered throwing John's body in the car and dumping it in one of the drug-infested neighborhoods of Miami, but that course of action involved even greater risks of being caught with a body where no explanation would be accepted by the authorities. He also knew that before they could call the police, he would have to move all his dope and paraphernalia to another location. This meant a fast trip back to the new apartment before the cops arrived.

"Maybe," he said to Gretchen, "we should just put him in the car and roll him out at some hospital."

"We can't do that," Gretchen screamed. "If that was me on the bed, would you dump me out like that?" Gripping Nick's arm, she insisted, "We've got to do the right thing. The police have to be called."

"Okay," Nick acknowledged, "but you'll have to stay here with the body while I get rid of all the dope."

"I can't do that," she responded flatly. "He died in our bed. I'm not sure I can stay here another night even if you're with me."

Gretchen's mother was at work, but her older half-brother was home for a visit. He wasn't into drugs, but he wasn't fond of cops either. He hadn't done anything illegal, he just didn't like cops, so Nick went over to Madeleine's house and asked him to come and stay with Gretchen. He explained what had happened and what he had to do before calling the police. Byron agreed, and Nick took off for Hollywood thanking his lucky stars he'd signed the lease and gotten the keys to their new place. The moment he returned, Gretchen called the police.

The ambulance arrived a few minutes ahead of the police, and once the paramedics saw John's body, with the tracks on his arms, they immediately classified his death as an O.D. That the police made the same assumption was reflected in the questions they asked. Nick and Gretchen answered with perfect innocence, but the police weren't completely satisfied. They took them all in for further questioning.

Byron wasn't involved and couldn't tell them anything, so they didn't bother much with him. They suspected Nick and Gretchen were into something, and grilled them for several hours. In the end, the police had to accept their story about going out for the afternoon, leaving John home alone and finding him dead when they returned. They couldn't prove otherwise and there was no evidence of drugs or paraphernalia at the apartment. They were all released without charges being filed. In truth, they were innocent. John had overdosed on his own, he just happened to do it at their place, and the business they were in made them susceptable to police suspicion.

The impact of John's death, however, had a lasting effect on both Nick and Gretchen. It didn't stop them from using drugs, but it did make them aware of the personal danger involved in their individual habits. Gretchen was hit the hardest and a tiny tendril of thought began to form that just maybe God was beginning to touch her life. Madeleine had planted this thought in her own deliberate way and it began to grow in Gretchen's brain.

Overdose deaths are not unusual among hard drug addicts. This hadn't been Nick's first encounter with an O.D. There had been another that had hit him with even greater impact. He'd gone to high school with Billy and they'd shot dope together. At one time, Billy had kicked his habit, but faced with temptation he'd weakened and gone back to the needle.

While overseas, Billy had taken a bullet in the hip, which doctors had been unable to remove. He'd been clean for almost a year, but the pain from that bullet was constant and almost unbearable. This may have been the reason he wanted the needle again. He knew what heroin could do, and if it eased his suffering and gave him a little rest from the pain, he'd accept addiction. At least this is how Nick's thoughts ran when he learned of Billy's death.

There's another side to O.D. deaths, however, and it's seldom considered by the authorities. Once a hard drug habit is kicked, the temptation remains. Every former addict will confirm this because, without God's help, it's too easy to fall again. Every addict who has gone through the terrors of withdrawal will also confirm that re-addiction is the same as slavery. Death is often regarded as the only way out. Therefore many O.D. deaths should be considered suicides. They aren't accidental, and for the persons involved, death may have seemed the only means of escape.

This may have been the case with both Billy and John. Billy couldn't live with the pain, and John didn't want to live as an addict. Their deaths, though painful to him, didn't stop Nick's desire for heroin. Perhaps that's the reason addicts always classify overdose deaths as being accidental. They simply can't accept the reality that they've enslaved themselves to a thoughtless, chemical master. They like to think of themselves as wise, daring, adventurous, fun-loving people who are *hip* to the good life and above the tribulations of the common folks. They have to keep reassuring themselves of this in order to escape the temptation of suicide.

Whenever a person surrenders himself, or herself, to a demanding chemical master, that person ceases to be a thinking, creative human being. An addict can't be trusted, believed or loved because he, or she, will sacrifice anything and everything for the momentary rush of the addiction. There is nothing in them to admire because their self-imposed loss of reality and dignity precludes their ability to admire themselves. Drug addiction is the ultimate defeating love/hate relationship that anyone can impose on himself. It's the epitome of selfish, senseless, self-defeating stupidity.

When an addict finally convinces himself that death is the only means of escape from chemical slavery, he adds idiocy to his stupidity, because there is another way. Escape can be achieved by simply changing masters. In order to understand this, the addict must realize that every living person serves a master. Each of us serves either God or Satan. Some think they are serving themselves, but that is a fallacy because either God or Satan is ruling their lives.

Neither Gretchen nor Nick understood this. God was not part of their lives and they considered Satan a funny man in a red suit with a forked tail. They both knew what they were doing was wrong, but as long as it served their purpose they thought they were serving themselves. This led them to an even greater fallacy. They actually believed they were in control of everything they did. It wasn't until later that they learned Satan was living in the house with them.

Yes, Death is a silent visitor, but so are God and Satan. Angels and demons can also come in silence. Any number of spirits can move in and influence a person's life without that person ever knowing they are present. With all the money rolling in, Gretchen and Nick were totally unaware of what had rolled in with it. She was the first to feel its evil presence through an overpowering sense of depression. When she lost interest in everything, Nick couldn't understand why. He was constantly on the go, expanding his business and improving his connections while Gretchen remained at home doing nothing. This went on for several months before he finally decided to find out what was wrong. He wanted an answer and firmly resolved not to settle for her usual reply.

They were watching television one evening when he got out of his chair and turned off the set. She didn't seem to notice what he'd done, so he asked, "Honey, what's the matter? Have I done something to upset you?"

"It's nothing," she answered.

"I can't accept that," he said, turning his chair to face hers and leaning forward. "You've been down in the dumps for months and there has to be a reason."

"It's nothing important," she repeated. "I just don't feel satisfied by what we're doing."

"We've got everything we want, plenty of money, the best dope in the world, fancy clothes and a nice car. We live in a fancy house with plenty of room and eat in the very best restaurants."

"I know," she admitted plaintively, "and maybe that's my problem. I feel down and there doesn't seem to be any purpose in my life. I used to think up ways to get a bag of dope or to make money we needed to live, but now I don't even have to do that."

"Would you feel better if I gave it all up?"

"No," she replied flatly.

"Then what can I do to make you feel better?"

"I don't know," she murmured. "I've spent the last thirty days just lying here on the couch. Today, I called the pizza parlor and had them deliver a glass of iced tea. I could have fixed it for myself, but I didn't want to be bothered. The kid who delivered it was amazed."

"Why?"

"The iced tea cost ninety cents," she said, "and I paid him with a ten dollar bill. He didn't complain or say anything, of course, but he must have thought I was nuts when I told him to keep the change." She rested her eyes on his as she whispered, "Nick, there's something here in the house that wants to hurt me. I can feel its evil presence in that back room where you keep the money and dope."

"Honey," Nick said, thinking he knew the cause of Gretchen's depression, "you must have got some bad dope. Give me your stash and I'll replace it with some good stuff. I'll fix you a spoon of..."

She stopped him by raising her hand. "No, Nick, that isn't it. I tried some of our best and my body couldn't take it. All I did was vomit and vomit." She smiled weakly and added, "Maybe I've had too much and my system just won't tolerate heroin any longer. It's either that or there is something in that back room that wants to destroy me."

"Gretchen, you're just tired," Nick reasoned, trying to comfort her. "Relax, darling, and I'll take you out for a good dinner. All you need is a change of scenery and a few laughs to make you feel better."

They went out that night, but it didn't change Gretchen's attitude about the back room. Her depression grew stronger as weeks passed. She lost a lot of weight and Nick's concern increased when she reached eighty pounds of skin and bones. She also had stopped going to the bathroom unless Nick was there to go with her because the bathroom adjoined the room she feared.

Coming home from an afternoon of business one day, Nick found her sitting on the living room couch in tears. She was shaking with fear, overwhelmed by the need to relieve herself, but afraid to go down the hallway alone.

"Gretchen," Nick insisted, "you've got to get a firm hold on yourself. This is ridiculous. I can't be here all the time and there's nothing in that room that's doing to harm you."

"Yes there is," she retorted bitterly. "Satan's in

that room counting all our evil money and cursing all our dope. I can feel him in there, and when he's through counting, I know he's coming after me."

Nick took her to the bathroom and waited until she was finished. When she was once again seated safely on the living room couch, he marched back to the dope room, unlocked the door and went in. For the first time, he felt a chill creep up his spine and he knew Gretchen was right. There was something evil in that room. It wasn't something physical, but rather like the cold breath of a silent visitor. In that instant, Nick was overpowered by the thought of how many people in Florida had overdosed on drugs from that room.

Gretchen felt the evilness in the dope room.

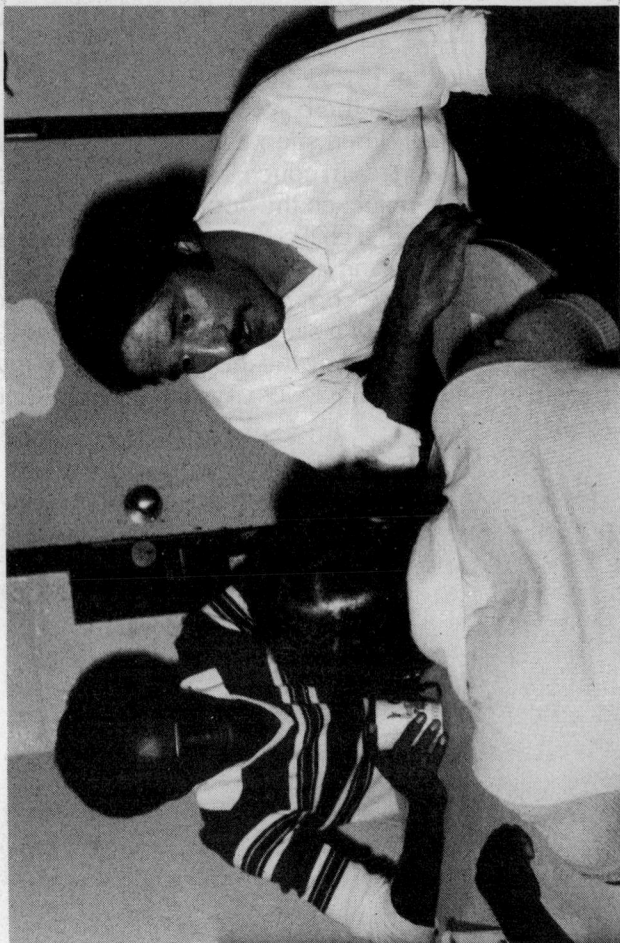

Nick spent
quite a bit
of time in jail.

90

JAIL-TIME BREAKS
THE PATTERN

*"Change was his mistress,
Chance was his counselor."*
Theodore Goodridge Roberts
(1885 - 1963)

Knowing he had to get the business out of the house to relieve the tension and depression Gretchen was experiencing, Nick began exploring other possibilities. He was also aware of the constant danger having drugs in the house posed for them if there should be a sudden police raid. Nick's father knew what he was doing and he was certain the Fort Lauderdale police were beginning to pay more attention to his activities.

His arrests on minor drug-related charges had resulted in short periods of county jail time and these were beginning to add up to a rather impressive accumulation of time behind bars. He didn't like the idea of Gretchen being left with a room full of dope and money in the event of his prolonged absence. He didn't want her dealing while he was locked up, and his dealers would expect her to keep them supplied if she had access to his drug inventory. For these reasons, he hired a young woman without a police record and paid her $400 a week to run the *cut-house*.

The *cut-house* was an apartment in Ft. Lauderdale. No one lived there and it was used exclusively for the storage and cutting of heroin that came in from Central America. A fake electronics company was established to provide cover for the operation. The girl was on call 24 hours a day, seven days a week. It was her job to pick up all their shipments at U.S. Customs and deliver them to the *cut-house*. She also did the cutting and packaging for resale.

The dope would arrive packed in containers of electronic equipment. Debbie would put magnetic "Field Electronic" signs on her van, slip into a Field Electronic tee shirt and pick it up after it cleared customs. She would then cut it eight times with lactose and package it in plastic bags of one-ounce and quarter-pound sizes. This stuff, mainly from Honduras, was so pure that it could be cut again before it hit the streets. Even with these cuts, people were killing themselves on accidental overdoses because of its strength.

With the dope out of the house, Gretchen's attitude slowly began to change. Her depression lightened and she began taking interest in life again, and both she and Nick were much less aware of an evil presence in the things they were doing. Their discernment was being dulled and they began overlooking things that they and others did which were not entirely normal. They began doing foolish things that they wouldn't have dreamed of doing just three or four years earlier. Their addiction to heroin was beginning to demand greater risks and exposure to greater danger.

A perfect example of this is the way Gretchen broke the usual pattern of their lives when she needed a fix while Nick was a 30-day guest at the County Jail. She had never personally sold dope, but her at-home supply was exhausted, and she knew where heroin was available, having gone with Nick on some of his deals. She didn't have access to the *cut-house*, but if she had, she wouldn't have gone there. That was where the evil spirit had gone when it left and she wanted nothing to do with it. Money was no problem, however, so she hit the streets looking for a buy.

Driving their Lincoln Continental into the black ghetto, Gretchen presented a very pretty picture. She was well dressed, obviously well heeled, alone and very attractive. As she slowly cruised the streets, looking for a familiar black face from one of Nick's deals, every man she passed made an effort to attract her attention. Spotting a fancy-dressed dude, the mark of either a pusher or a pimp, she pulled over and parked the car.

Rolling down the car window, she called to him. "Can you help me?" she asked with an engaging smile.

"Hey, pretty lady," he chortled, swaggering to the car, "I'm your man. What can I do for you?"

She really didn't know how to ask if he was a pusher, but she needed the dope and had to take a chance. "I'm looking for something special," she confided. "Something that'll make me feel good."

"Like what?" he pressed, grinning broadly. "If it's a real man you're looking for to change your luck, you've found him."

"No, no," she said, smiling to soften her rejection of his sexual offer. "I'm looking to buy a little dope."

He understood immediately. "How much and what do you want?"

"I want heroin," she told him frankly, "and I'll take all you've got."

"Hold on, baby," he said, giving her and the car an appraisal, "I can get all you want, but I don't carry it around in my pocket."

"Can you go get it?"

"Sure," he admitted, "but you're such a pretty little thing, maybe you'd like to come with me. We could get the dope and have a little party. Then you

93

could go home feeling real good."

"How long would it take you to get the stuff?"

"About five minutes," he answered.

"Get it," she snapped. "I'll wait here."

"I've got to have the money first," he said.

"How much?"

"Five big ones," he replied.

Opening her purse, Gretchen peeled off five hundred dollars. She thought the man might know Nick or recognize the car. If that were the case, she felt certain he wouldn't try to rip her off. Nick's reputation for violence was fairly well known and very few people tried fooling around with him, but she still played it cautiously.

Holding the cash up where he could see it, she said, "Look, you know I've got the money, so why don't you just go get the stuff and then I'll give you the cash."

"No, lady, that ain't the way it's done down here," he insisted. "I take your money and buy the dope, then I bring it back to you. The money always comes first."

"Is it good stuff?" she asked to cover her reluctance to trust him.

"The best," he bragged. "Give me the money and I'll take good care of it and you."

Gretchen handed him the cash, but the moment he started to walk away, she knew it had been a mistake. He turned and looked back at her just before entering an old, run down building. "Hey, pretty lady," he shouted, "thanks for the donation!" He was laughing as he disappeared into the darkened, rat-infested hallway.

Quickly rolling the window back up, she yanked the car keys out of the ignition, opened the door, got out, jammed the lock button down and slammed it closed. She needed a fix, but her anger momentarily overcame that. All she wanted to do was catch the

94

bum, get her money back and change the tone of his voice with a sharp kick to the groin. Gretchen felt absolutely no fear as she ran into the strange building. She was 108 pounds of feminine fury as she charged down that dark hallway.

Nick would have hesitated to do what she was doing. This wasn't the neighborhood for an attractive woman to enter alone. It was the bottom of the human barrel and the people living there had to scratch and fight just to stay alive. The man, if she had caught him, could have killed her easily, and with tracks on her arms, the police might have listed her death as drug-related and never tried to catch her killer. Even if she were raped, before or after death, it could have remained just another unsolved drug-related murder.

After pounding on a few doors with no response, she finally decided she'd been a fool and returned to the car. As she drove out of the neighborhood, she spotted a man she knew Nick had dealt with. He recognized the car when she stopped. Five minutes later, Gretchen was on her way home with four *nickel* bags of heroin in her purse as she played one of her favorite tapes on the car's tape player.

Turning up the volume, she sang along with *Savoy Brown* as the words of *Needle and Spoon* filled the car. "To some I'm a wise man," she sang, "and to some I'm a fool, but I need a little something just to keep my cool. I sleep with the sun and I rise with the moon, and I feel so good with my needle and spoon." She wasn't thinking of the danger she'd been in. She wasn't concerned about the money she'd lost. She had forgotten her fear of the evil spirit. All that concerned her was the rush she'd get from her needle and spoon. The music suited her mood and she knew Nick would be out in just four more days, so she could relax and enjoy the high she would soon be feeling.

In her heart, Gretchen knew what she was doing was wrong, but the song seemed to justify her craving for heroin. It glorified the *delights* of the needle and spoon and told the world that heroin was the answer. Wasn't the fact that such a song could be recorded and sold proof that heroin was okay? It made her feel comfortable and part of the action by telling her that she wasn't alone in her addiction. It encouraged her to continue seeking heroin's seductive promise by mainlining her habit. For those who were not yet hooked, the song held out the invitation and promise that heroin was the ultimate trip to eternal *joy* and *peace.* It was the music of a false promise and the harmony for a tormented soul.

There were other times when Nick's absence broke his business pattern. He didn't really have to be gone long for the breakdown to appear, even a ten-day stay in the county jail could produce dramatic results. After one such period of county hospitality, Nick came out to find the *cut-house* empty and all his dealers and their pushers dry. He and Gretchen were both hurting. They desperately needed the fix they could only get from heroin. Marijuana was like putting a paper patch on a flat tire, so they were forced to make a run to his connection in Miami.

This wasn't in keeping with Nick's normal pattern, but it was a risk they had to take. Nick was too far gone to drive. His skin was crawling over tight bone joints and the backs of his eyes were on fire. Gretchen was in a little better shape. It hadn't been ten days since her last fix, so she got behind the wheel of their big Lincoln and headed for the freeway. It was early morning, traffic was light, and they were in a hurry. She was doing 85 in the faint light of dawn when the car betrayed them.

As with his motorcycle, Nick had never read the car's operating manual. The oil had never been changed or checked. As the machine faltered,

Gretchen looked in the rearview mirror and shouted at Nick who was lying across the back seat.

"Nick, look behind us!" she yelled.

Painfully raising his head, he mumbled, "What happened? Where'd all the smoke come from?"

"I don't know," she answered in exasperation as the car coasted to a stop at the side of the freeway. "The motor just stopped running."

"Are you out of gas?"

"No!" she exclaimed.

"Try to start it again," he instructed impatiently. "We've got to get to Miami. I can't take this much longer."

She turned the key in the ignition. Nothing happened. The starter couldn't turn the engine. It had seized up and frozen, low on oil. The car was less than eight months old. It was the best car Ford Motor Company made. The warranty was still good on it. Nick's anger exploded. He cursed the machine and the men who'd made it. He called them every foul name he could think of. Gretchen joined him in this litany of hate as they decided to leave the car and hitchhike into Miami. They didn't care if they ever saw the car again. All they wanted was a fix, and once that had been obtained, they'd buy a new Lincoln for the drive back to Fort Lauderdale.

They caught a ride to the next freeway exit and were dropped off at a Shell station which wasn't scheduled to open for an hour. There was, however, a phone booth they could use to call for help. Nick dialed the number of a business friend, got him out of bed, told him what they needed and where they were.

"I'll get there as fast as I can," he said.

"Bring something with you," Nick demanded. "We're hurting bad!"

"Okay," the man promised. "Just sit tight; I'm on my way."

They were both rolling around on the pavement in total agony by the time he arrived. The service station opened just as Nick and Gretchen got into the friend's car and eagerly accepted the rush of the needle and spoon.

They had reached a critical point in their lives, where heroin was the god they worshipped. It was their total master. They were willing and ready to sacrifice everything for it. Their human dignity was gone. It meant nothing to them without heroin. Money meant nothing to them except for its value in exchange for the dope they needed. Friendship, loyalty, truth, and life itself no longer had any meaning beyond what they could gain from the needle and spoon. The love they had for each other was still intact. It couldn't be destroyed, but neither Nick or Gretchen was aware of this, or concerned about it as they proceeded to do everything in their power to kill it. They were engulfed in their addiction and nothing else mattered, but they still refused to admit it even to themselves.

Continuing to think they were in complete control of what they were doing, they gave themselves over to the demands of their chosen master. If greater violence was demanded, they gave it. If greater risks were required, they took them. They lost count of time. Days and months passed in their drug induced haze. The evil which Gretchen thought was locked in the *cut-house* had come out and crept into them both. That spirit wasn't alone. It came with companions and introduced them to Nick and Gretchen as helpers and fellow travelers.

"These are friends of mine," the spirit whispered evilly. "Work with them. Trust them. They can show you great things and teach you my ways."

Neither Nick nor Gretchen actually heard the spirit tell them this, but they obeyed the demands of their god and witnessed the malignancy of the message's meaning. Neither of them would admit the existence of demons or devils, but they worked and played with other slaves of the *dark master*. If Satan had appeared, suddenly, and shouted his orders, they would have obeyed willingly.

DEMONS AND STRANGERS

"You may be a man of sorrows, and on speaking terms with Care, and as yet be unacquainted with The Demon of Despair."

Henry Lawson
(1867 - 1922)

Their craving temporarily satisfied, Nick easily slipped back into the old pattern and began to function again. He resupplied the *cut-house* and filled the pipeline to his dealers, but something had been added to the process that he didn't comprehend. A new face had suddenly become involved, not as competition, but as an addition to the pattern without actually being part of Nick's operation. Gretchen felt this influence first, then Nick saw it manifested in the helpful, but unrequested, activities of a man named Tom Greene.

Tom was a stranger to everyone Nick knew. At first he thought Tom might be a *narc*, seeking to entrap him in some way, but all inquiries into his background produced nothing negative. Tom's apparent knowledge of Nick's operation seemed to indicate that if he were a *narc*, he could have blown the whistle on Nick without any further effort. In addition to this, Tom was a user and involved in some minor deals of his own. On the surface, it seemed he only wanted to help Nick make more money and get a little of it for himself. Gretchen was aware of Tom, but when Nick accepted him, she turned her concern back to the danger she'd felt in the house.

Having felt that evil presence in the house, and not being sure what it really was, Gretchen was intrigued by the mystery of it. She wanted to know more about where it came from, why it had been there, where it had gone, what its purpose was, and who it was. Heroin had sublimated her need to know the purpose of her life, but it hadn't erased her youthful curiosity or removed her desire for understanding the things that influenced her life. There were times when she savored melancholy feelings and enjoyed listening to music that projected a morbid hopelessness.

Savoy Brown's song, *Life's A One Act Play,* held great appeal for her. Unaware of the real meaning of life, Gretchen found great solace in the song's lyrics, yet something deep inside her refused to accept the finality of the song's message. Something kept telling her there was more to life than just the time we spend here on earth. She was young, not yet 20, and didn't want to think that what she had was all she was going to get out of having been born. At the same time, the song pleased her by providing a rationale that seemed to justify her need to get high and do whatever felt good. That wasn't what she really wanted to believe, and she had to find out if it was true.

How can I be frightened of spirits I can't see, Gretchen thought, *if there isn't something beyond the life I'm living? There must be more to all this and I've got to find out what it is. Why can I feel the presence of evil and still not understand the reason I'm alive? I thought heroin had solved this for me. Why did that feeling of evil bring it back?*

These questions plagued Gretchen, even when she was high, because they were stimulated by a power directly related to the heroin she craved. In letting her feel its evilness, the spirit in that back bedroom had betrayed itself by creating doubts in

Gretchen's mind. She had been more than ready to accept the premise of only living one life because she could see nothing beyond it, but the spirit's presence showed her there was more for her to learn.

Anyone who experiences the spirits of fear, joy, sadness, happiness, anger or peace, is an absolute fool if he or she continues to believe that life is only a one-time process. None of these feelings can be seen, but they do exist and they're real. The spirit of evil and the spirit of good are both present in all our lives, and anyone who denies their existence has to believe in them or there would be nothing to deny. Gretchen was not a fool. She knew there was a spirit world, but she didn't know how to reach it or understand it. In her search for more knowledge, she turned to the occult, thinking it might be the doorway to the ultimate truth.

As with most people, particularly those with an adventurous and creative mind, Gretchen felt a pull toward the mysterious and secretive practices of the occult. She and her friend Kathy often played with the Ouija board. They were both aware of God, but it wasn't a personal awareness. They were both aware of Satan, but here again, they didn't relate their lives to him. God and Satan were just two concepts that really didn't personally apply to them. They wanted something they could see as well as feel and the Ouija board was something they could touch with their hands. It was an easy way for the spirit world to reveal itself to them.

Facing each other across the table in Gretchen's kitchen one afternoon, they put their hands on the board's planchette and asked the questions that were puzzling them. They couldn't understand the board's answer. It spelled out *Zelda*. They asked the question again and the board repeated the same answer. Neither of them knew a Zelda, but they didn't discard the answer, or the board, thinking they might meet this Zelda and then the board's meaning would be made clear to them. Gretchen put the board away, and they went shopping. She wasn't prepared for the strange happenings that ensued.

When they returned to the house, Gretchen gave Kathy her packages to hold while she took the door keys from her purse. Trying the key in the lock, she exclaimed, "Someone's changed the locks! My key doesn't work!"

"Here," Kathy said, "you hold the packages and let me try."

The key still failed to unlock the door and Gretchen observed, "It worked earlier today, and we've only been gone a couple of hours. Nick didn't say anything about changing the locks." Putting the packages down, she took the key from Kathy and tried again. The door remained locked. "Wait here," she said to her friend, "I'll run around to the back door and see if I can get in that way."

The key didn't work there either. Returning to the front door, upset that Nick could have changed locks without telling her, she angrily jammed the key in the lock once more. It turned with the greatest of ease and the door swung open effortlessly. Pondering this as they entered the house, Gretchen experienced the strange feeling that they had been kept outside until someone was through doing what had to be done in the house. It was as if they'd nearly interrupted something they were not supposed to see or know about.

Putting the packages down on the kitchen counter, she turned to express this feeling to Kathy when she noticed the Ouija board on the table where they had been playing. Thinking, *I put that board away. How did it get back out? What's going on here?* she said, "Kathy, I put that thing away and now it's back out on the table."

Kathy's eyes widened in surprise as she saw the

104

board. "Yes, you put it on the shelf in the front closet."

"Something's going on here that I don't like," Gretchen whispered. "I think it's time for us to get rid of the Ouija board."

"Yes," Kathy agreed wholeheartedly.

The board was immediately relegated to the garbage. They didn't know it should have been burned and destroyed. As a result of this omission, the mysterious appeal of the occult stayed with them.

On their shopping trips to Miami, Gretchen and Kathy were invariably drawn to a specific street and a particular address. It was the house of a man named Vandecar, a self-proclaimed Satanist. He ran personal ads in the Miami newspapers inviting the public to visit his home and experience the wonders of the Satanic religion.

Both girls were fascinated by the statues of demons and evil spirits that could be seen in the front yard. According to the ads, it was an open house and anyone could enter. One evening, as they stood on the sidewalk in front of the house, a man approached them from behind.

"Good evening, ladies," he said politely. "I'm going inside; would you like to join me?"

"What's in there?" Kathy blurted.

"Yes, what goes on inside?" Gretchen asked.

"Come in and see for yourselves," the man invited. "Once inside, you'll be pleasantly surprised because you'll find your own likeness someplace in the house. It's a confirming sign for all who enter that this is where you belong. No one will harm you in any way and you may learn the truth about yourselves and be blessed by the dark master."

This was too much for them to resist. Both Gretchen and Kathy followed the man up the front steps. They were nervous and apprehensive as they crossed the threshold. They felt as if the house threatened them. They didn't stay long enough to look for their likenesses. They didn't meet Vandecar or experience any of the promised truth, but they revealed their interest in the occult and exposed themselves to further exploitation.

On the drive back to Fort Lauderdale, Gretchen rationalized, "Kathy, there must be something to the Satanic religion. That man, the one who took us inside the house, he may have been Vandecar, but if he wasn't, then he was a believer and an advocate of Satan's power and reality."

"I don't know about any of that," Kathy replied, "but I never want to go back there again. I've never been so uncomfortable in my life as I was inside that place."

"Yeah," Gretchen agreed thoughtfully. "I know what you mean."

That night, Gretchen didn't tell Nick anything about the strange house in Miami. It didn't occur to her that he might be interested. During dinner, he told her about Tom Greene's escape from a dangerous situation. She didn't connect Tom with the evil spirit, even when Nick told her how Tom always managed to avoid any form of trouble or personal danger. She didn't make the connection until a great deal later.

As the weeks passed, Gretchen and Kathy continued to flirt with the mystery of the occult. Smoking *joints* while watching afternoon reruns of *Bewitched* on television, they'd try to imagine what it would be like to possess the powers Elizabeth Montgomery demonstrated in the show. They were attractive young women and in their daydreams they could fantasize about being beautiful witches. They also were fascinated by the movie, *Bell, Book and Candle,* as it extolled the magic of another beautiful witch. In time, their fantasies seemed to become reality. There were times, especially when they were using drugs, when they genuinely felt they possessed the powers they'd seen demonstrated. It amused

106

them to manipulate the people around them for their own enjoyment. It was all just a game, and they were unaware of the hidden danger.

Gretchen finally became concerned when she realized it was affecting her relationship with Nick. He didn't play the game and she found it difficult to identify what was fantasy and what was real when she was with him. It didn't help when he told her about Tom Greene's final disappearance.

"Honey," he related to Gretchen while getting dressed for his shift at the radio station, "Tom and a guy named Mark were trying to make a deal on a large quantity of reefer with a man from Miami. The man didn't know either of them, and wouldn't trust them, so they brought me in on the deal. The guy knew and would trust me, so I called him and set it up.

"Tom figured we'd get the guy to bring his money into a remote neighborhood, then rip him off. It was good money and a good plan, so I went along with it. I picked the guy up and drove out to this dark area and parked the car. I told him we'd have to walk down the street to a house about 200 yards away. He got out of the car on his side and I got out on mine. When I joined him on his side, I jammed my gun in his face and told him to get on his knees.

"He was on his knees when Tom took his money. I told him to get up, turn around and walk away. I warned him not to look back unless he wanted to be shot. As he walked into the darkness, we took off and divided the take. Later, this guy and his friends caught Tom and Mark in an old building on the other side of town. As they threw down on them and demanded their money back, Tom vanished.

"The story I get from people in the know is that Tom flew right up through an old skylight and disappeared. They got Mark and another guy that was with them, but they let the other guy go to tell me

107

they wanted the money I got from the deal.

"They're dragging Mark all around town, showing everybody what happens to someone who tries to rip them off. They've really done a number on Mark. His face has been burned with cigarettes and he's been beaten half to death. They want me and Tom to come in and give 'em back the money, but nobody knows where to find Tom. I've got to get somebody to take my shift at the station, then I'm going down to Hollywood and hide out for a few days. I'll get word back to them so they won't come here looking for me, but don't let anyone you don't know in the house."

"Are you going to give them their money?" Gretchen questioned.

"I don't want to," Nick answered, "but I might have to. I'll see how it all comes down before I decide. If Tom ever shows up, I'll do whatever he decides to do, because if we don't, they'll just go on hurting Mark. They may even eventually kill him."

"Then let them have it back," Gretchen urged. "We don't need it and if it'll save Mark a lot of pain, let 'em have it."

"Yeah," Nick agreed, "I may have to do that, but I'd like to hear from Tom first." He studied Gretchen for a moment before adding, "He went up through that skylight like magic. It doesn't make any sense. It's spooky and I don't like it. Tom just popped into our lives from out of nowhere and now he's popped right back out without a trace. He must be some kind of devil or something."

Gretchen had already thought of that possibility, but she didn't say anything to Nick at that particular moment. She wasn't sure about Tom, but she knew demons could disappear and reappear without the slightest problem, and if Tom turned out to be a demon, she wasn't sure how much she wanted to know about it.

108

"Nick, please be careful," she warned, "there's an awful lot of things happening right now that don't make any sense, so don't push your luck."

"I'll be careful," he agreed, leaving the house.

Nick never saw or heard from Tom again. The people they'd ripped off passed the word that if Nick would give up his share of the dough, they'd back off without taking any further action. Nick didn't believe them. They wanted him to meet them at the giant water slide on Dania Beach and return their money. It was a public place, crowded with people, but he still didn't trust them. He made a plan of his own instead.

Finding a girl who wasn't connected with him in any way, Nick paid her to bury the money on the beach. When this was done, he called and let them know where they could find it. That ended that matter, but the mystery of Tom Greene remained. No one knew anything about him and no one ever saw him again. He vanished completely, and Nick began to wonder if Tom was really what he seemed to be. This possibility grew stronger in his mind when Gretchen speculated that he might have been a demon sent to destroy them. Nick wasn't ready to completely accept this idea, but he held it in reserve as a possible explanation.

A few weeks later, the idea made a little more sense when he began receiving strange phone calls while on the air. Gretchen was with him the night the calls started. Nick would have passed them off as mere crank calls if things hadn't started happening that forced him to acknowledge the truth of the threats they contained.

Gretchen loved to sit in the broadcast booth and watch Nick work. He looked so cool and in control as he announced the records and played the commercials. She was fascinated by the way he cued up each song and held the turntable until it was time for the music. Then he'd relax and talk to her while the music played. As if by magic, he always seemed to know when it was time to get back on the mike and talk to his listeners.

He'd just started a record spinning when the light on the phone began blinking. He picked it up, expecting a listener requesting some favorite, but without preamble, a deep male voice said, "I'm going to pull your station's broadcast power. I've got my house set up as a station and I'm pulling your power right now."

Nick's eyes immediately shot to the VU meter which registered the 50,000 watts of their signal. It was falling. The station was losing its signal. "Can you dig what's happening?" the voice chortled.

"Who are you?" Nick demanded. "Where are you?"

The only reply he heard was a low laugh and the click of a broken connection. He knew the station was located in an open field at the end of a rural country road. There were no houses within almost a mile. The station power was supplied on underground lines that were completely inaccessible to outside interference. There was no way for anyone to pull their signal, but it was happening. As he continued to yell into a dead phone, the signal's strength began climbing back to normal. Gretchen's nervous laughter joined Nick's as he tried to understand what had happened. Neither of them laughed very long, however, when the phone rang a second time and the voice was back.

"That's was just a taste of what I can do," the voice whispered. "Now, I'm going to pull it all away and knock you off the air!"

Once again Nick watched the meter drop, but this time it dropped to the bottom. The station completely lost its broadcast power. It was silent. As they say in the trade, "The station went dark."

Doing everything he could to restore the signal,

110

Nick was helpless. Nothing worked. He had never been in a position like this before. His training at the broadcast school covered just such an emergency, but the back-up power source, a separate independent generator, failed to respond. He was about to go check the outside connections when the VU meter once again climbed back to normal. Breathing a deep sigh of relief, he returned to broadcasting and while the next record was spinning, he noted the station's power failure in the broadcast log. The day shift could search out the cause when there were more people around to handle the problem.

At the end of the shift, he told his relief what had happened and headed for the car. It was still dark outside as Nick helped Gretchen into the car. As he closed her door and started around to the driver's side, a man approached from out of the darkness.

"Can you dig what happened?" he asked with a knowing smile.

"Hey," Nick yelled, "the FCC will want to talk to..." There was no sense trying to continue. Nick and Gretchen were the only people in the parking lot. Blinking his eyes, Nick began to doubt that he'd gotten the phone calls or seen the man coming toward them. Gretchen dispelled this idea when he joined her in the car.

"Who was that guy?" she asked. "Does he work here at the station?" Sliding across the seat, she snuggled up to Nick as she murmured, "Let's go home. I'm afraid to think of what's happening to us. Maybe all of this will make sense after a little sleep."

Gretchen was certain she and Nick were being harassed by evil demons. She was sure there could be no other explanation, and now she had another demon to contend with. It was the demon of deep despair and she felt helpless because she didn't know how to fight it.

111

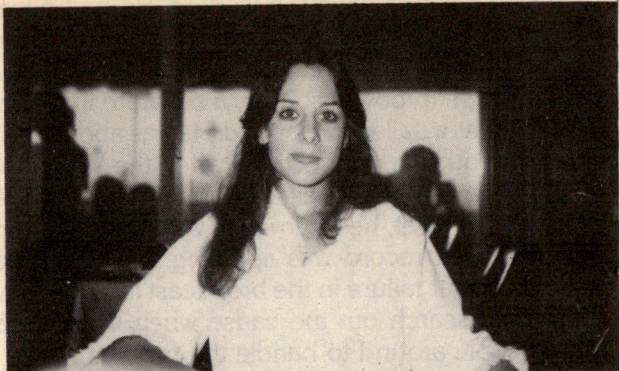

Gretchen thought of quitting drugs
when she was "high".

Nick thought he was in control
of his life, but heroin was.

FACING REALITY

*"The use of living is to regulate imagination
by reality, and instead of thinking how things
may be, to see them as they are."*

Samuel Johnson
(1709 - 1784)

Attempting to understand what was happening
to them, Gretchen was forced to admit the only thing
of value in their lives was the love she and Nick
shared. Their addiction kept growing and placing a
greater burden on their resources. The heroin their
bodies demanded, even at the prices Nick paid,
demanded an expenditure of almost $5,000 every
week. Aside from other living expenses, they needed
$260,000 every year just to pacify their craving. The
impact of this hit her when she realized that need
would never go away until it killed them or they broke
the habit.

It was easy to think of quitting while she was high,
but when she needed a fix, it was the last thing in the
world she could imagine herself doing. Her craving
overruled all other thoughts. Gretchen realized if
anything ever happened to Nick, she'd have to face
her habit alone. That was a terror she couldn't
accept. The very thought of it filled her with an
overwhelming fear that made her more dependent
on Nick and the love he gave her.

Gretchen loved Nick beyond life itself. Heroin had
nothing to do with that, it was simply a by-product of

Nick and his daughter, Lisa

Nick, though addicted, could still feel Lisa's trusting love.

their relationship, something they did together. This was her frame of mind when he finally told her he was married and introduced her to Lisa, his six-year old daughter. She never questioned why he'd kept the secret from her and she accepted Lisa with the same love she felt for him. It was a fact she couldn't change and it didn't affect her feelings for Nick.

Lisa, however, was another element to be accommodated in their relationship. Whenever Nick's wife permitted Lisa to spend entire days or even weekends with her father, both Nick and Gretchen were more circumspect in their drug-related activities. They tried to conceal their addiction to heroin, and cut back on their use of marijuana, but there were times when the need for a fix overrode their caution. With youthful curiosity, Lisa often questioned what they were doing.

One afternoon, after shooting-up in the bathroom, Nick emerged to face his puzzled daughter. She was too young to fully understand what he'd done, but her question made him stop and think about his lifestyle. It also made an impression on Gretchen's conscience.

"Daddy," she asked seriously, "why are you so sick when you go into the bathroom, and not sick any more when you come out?"

This was a question he couldn't answer truthfully, so he lied. "I take some special medicine that makes me feel better."

"When I'm sick," she pressed, "will you give me some of your medicine and make me better, too?"

"Honey," he lied again, "it's a grownup sickness and I hope you'll never need it."

"Even when I'm big like you?"

Wanting to get Nick off the hook, Gretchen answered for him. "Lisa," she explained, "people don't get sick the same way, and if you're a good girl, you'll never need your daddy's medicine." Changing

115

the subject, Gretchen looked at Nick and asked, "Didn't you promise to take us out for ice cream?"

"Yeah," he replied. "We'll go down to Baskin-Robbins and try all 31 flavors if you girls think you can eat that much."

Later, on their way back to Fort Lauderdale after returning Lisa to her mother's, Nick made a surprising observation. "I've been thinking," he said, "that maybe it's time for us to get off this treadmill."

"What do you mean?" Gretchen asked.

"Maybe we should quit using," he answered.

This was the first time Nick had openly expressed such feelings and Gretchen wasn't sure if he was serious. They both knew that heroin was getting too strong a grip on them, but they both doubted they were strong enough to break that grip. The fact that neither of them really wanted to quit was the weakening factor in Nick's observation.

As Nick indicated to Gretchen during their arguments over starting her on heroin, he knew how vulnerable addicted women were to physical exploitation. Perhaps it was the thought that Lisa might someday be forced to submit herself to a pusher/pimp if she followed her daddy's example that made him think of quitting. It pained him deeply to think of his little girl hooked on heroin and selling her body just to obtain the drug he was promoting and selling.

Every time he saw Lisa's sweet face, heard her happy laughter and felt the warmth of her trusting love, he experienced a twinge of guilt over what his heroin could be doing to the daughters of other men. Nick didn't like this feeling, but as a slave to the drug himself, he felt powerless to stop.

Gretchen was also stung by the realization that Lisa's generation was vulnerable to the evil they were promoting. She understood the power of drug addiction and was well aware of what it was doing in their lives. When Nick indicated it might be time to withdraw, Gretchen agreed.

"Nick," she suggested seriously, "maybe we should check out the Methadone program that all the television people are talking about. They've got a clinic started at St. Luke's Hospital in Miami. It's not here in Ft. Lauderdale, so nobody would know us over there and we could check it out as just another couple wanting to dry out and clean up their lives."

"It's worth a try," he admitted. "I'd like to change and get the monkey off my back."

"Me, too," Gretchen agreed. "Our habits have gotten bigger than both of us and if the clinic can get us detoxed, I think we're strong enough to stay clean."

"Maybe," Nick concluded doubtfully. "Anyway, it's worth a try. There's a doctor in Miami by the name of Ben Shepherd. We'll go to him. I've heard that he has a heart for junkies and really wants to help. If he'll take us on, we'll have him put us in the program and supervise our treatment."

In making this decision, they'd admitted their need for help. That's half the battle, but from a physical standpoint, it's the easy half. According to the news reports and the television talk shows, methadone was the answer to heroin addiction. It was a legal substitute for an illegal drug, which could be administered to break the addict's need and then slowly withdrawn to effect a cure. Nick and Gretchen went to Dr. Shepherd with great expectations, hoping that all the stories they'd heard were correct.

Perhaps they were expecting too much from the program, or possibly Dr. Shepherd didn't adequately explain it to them, but Nick didn't stay with it for more than 60 days. He was still dealing heroin while in the program, and having it available may have influenced his actions. In any event, he was back where he started before the program could change his need.

On the other hand, Gretchen stayed with it for five

months before she realized they weren't detoxifying her. Her habit had been maintained on an extremely high dosage of methadone. When she expressed her concern over the length of the treatment and the dosage she was getting, the doctor questioned her desire.

"Do you really want to get off the methadone completely?" he asked.

"Yes," she answered adamantly.

"Then you'll have to be hospitalized. Is that what you want?"

"I want what ever it's going to take," she insisted.

"Very well," the doctor concluded, "I'll make arrangements for your admission to the South Miami Hospital and we'll start a schedule of treatments to get you through withdrawal and detoxification. It won't be easy, but if you really want to break your addiction, it's the only way to do it with any hope of success."

At this point, Gretchen wasn't aware that methadone addiction was equally as hard, if not harder, to break as heroin addiction. she entered the hospital with great expectations for a complete cure, but she wasn't prepared for what actually happened.

As requested, she was being detoxified, but her system was being loaded with other drugs in addition to the continued use of methadone. Mentally, Gretchen was slipping into periods of extremely bizarre behavior. Nick didn't like what was happening to her, so he would bring heroin with him on his visits and help her get off while he was with her. This added to her problems in ways the hospital staff couldn't understand and led them to increase the dosage of the drugs they were providing.

It soon became apparent that nothing was working as it should. Gretchen was out of control. When her mother came to see her, Gretchen threw her out of the room. This happened with all her other visitors as well.

118

Nick was the only person she allowed to stay for more than a few minutes, and eventually he, too, was rejected. In a true sense, her system was making her do the very things she needed to do for a cure. By discouraging all visitors, she was limiting her access to the heroin Nick had been providing and the hospital began getting some of the expected results from her schedule of treatment.

Over a period of several weeks, they actually got her detoxed down to a very small amount of drugs. Gretchen's mind began to clear and she was once again aware of where she was and what was happening to her. She reacted with a very independent spirit by walking out of the hospital after the final bed-check on a Friday night. She wasn't cured and wasn't well, but she felt better than she had in several weeks and wanted to go home.

As it happened, Nick had left for the weekend. He was making a delivery to his dealer at Disney World. Gretchen didn't know where he was, and when she started getting sick, in desperation she called her married sister who was living in California.

"Harree," she cried over the phone, "I just came home from the hospital and Nick isn't here. I don't know where he's gone and when he'll be back. I'm in withdrawal from drug addiction and I'm sick."

"Can't you go back to the hospital?" Harree asked sympathetically.

"No, no," Gretchen sobbed. "I can't take that any longer. It seems like I've just returned to the world of the living. They kept me doped up in there and I really didn't know what I was doing, or what they were doing to me. I don't want to go back!"

"Honey," Harree asked, "is there anything we can do for you? Is there anyone you want us to call to help you?"

Gretchen was trying to think of a reply, when Harree's husband got on the phone. "Gretchen," he offered, "I'll buy your plane ticket. It'll be at the American Airlines ticket desk at the Miami airport when you get there. Harree and I want you to come out here and stay with us. We'll go through whatever is necessary with you, whatever it takes to help you kick your habit. We love you, Gretchen, so please come and let us help you."

Gretchen felt hope come alive in her heart. His concern and tenderness had touched her. "I'll leave for the airport as soon as I can pack a bag. Will you meet me at the airport out there?"

"I'll find out when your flight arrives here from the airline," he answered, "and we'll be a waiting at the gate when you arrive. Don't worry about anything. We want you here with us where we can take care of you."

Getting sicker by the minute, Gretchen picked up her ticket and boarded the flight to California. It was her first trip to the West Coast, but her memory of it is clouded by the pain of withdrawal. She was coming off methadone, heroin was no longer involved, and her misery was magnified by being alone on the flight, unable to tell anyone what was wrong and not willing to ask for help.

Arriving at her destination, Gretchen welcomed her sister's embrace. It was a strange reunion. Harree hardly recognized her and immediately showed deep concern over her loss of weight and haggard appearance. They took Gretchen to their apartment and gave her what comfort they could in the form of love and support. She accepted this, but was still unable to really comprehend where she was or tell them what she needed. Withdrawing further inside herself, Gretchen tried to fight her pain and craving on her own.

"There must be something we can do to help you," Harree pleaded. "Tell us what it is and we'll do it."

Harree's voice sounded as if it were coming from the end of a long tunnel. Gretchen could hear her sister's love in what she was saying, but didn't know what to tell them. She tried to explain what was happening to her and how she felt, but having never experienced the pain themselves, they couldn't fully understand.

Gretchen spent eight terrible days in California. She tried to kill herself by slamming her head, repeatedly, on the sharp corner of their coffee table while Harree was out grocery shopping. John, Harree's husband, heard the noise and came running. He'd been up all night helping Gretchen, in spite of his heart condition, and was preparing to go to work. He found her bleeding and nearly unconscious. After stopping the bleeding, he got her into bed and stayed with her until Harree returned and took over. "Gretchen," Harree demanded to know while placing a cold compress on her bruised head, "what made you do this to yourself?"

Fighting her pain and shame, Gretchen sobbed, "I wanted to end my pain by killing myself. I can't take it any longer!"

"Honey, you can beat this thing," Harree said sympathetically, "but it's going to take time. I know it hurts, but you've got to give yourself a chance. All you've accomplished with this is to give yourself a massive headache."

"I know," Gretchen admitted with a grimace, "but while I was doing it, it hurt so much that I didn't feel the other pain."

"That doesn't make sense," Harree reasoned, "and you can't go on like this. We've got to take you to a doctor."

"No, no," Gretchen insisted. "I don't want any more doctors. It was my doctors that made me feel this way." Holding Harree's hands, she added, "I know you want to help me, but being here with you isn't the answer. I should go home where Nick can ride this out with me."

"If you go back," Harree asked, "will you stay off heroin?"

"Yes," Gretchen promised. "If it's humanly possible,

I intend to beat my habit."

Having made this promise, Gretchen was booked on a return flight to Florida. She called Nick and told him when she would arrive so he could meet her. Just talking to him made her feel a little better and the flight home was easier than her trip west, but she still had to face the fact that she wasn't free of her addiction. Heroin is not an easy master to beat, and methadone, if anything, is tougher.

After arriving home, Gretchen stayed clean for a month and a half. She did this on nerves alone. Nick was still dealing and using. She could have shot-up at any time, but she didn't.

During that 45 days, she didn't sleep. From a physical standpoint, Gretchen was winning the fight with her methadone addiction, but it was sapping all her strength. Her weight fell to seventy pounds, but her physical craving was gone. It was then that she was hit with the mental side of addiction. Her mind didn't seem to function. She was unable to think logically. Her thoughts ran together and then exploded in dozens of different directions at the same time. She couldn't find clothes that would fit, and when she looked for them, she would forget what she was seeking before she could find them.

On top of this, she and Nick were forced to face an additional facet of reality. His primary connection, his source for drugs, turned up dead. Even with Gretchen not using, his supply of heroin was dwindling fast. He could see the end, when he would have to buy on the open market for himself.

There was also another element to be considered. Never a day went by that Nick didn't see police activity around their house. He knew they were closing in on him, purposely showing themselves to make him aware of their constant surveillance. He had to restrict his actions and this made him think of getting clean himself. Both he and his friend, Rick, decided it was time to make the break. Gretchen was beginning to recover her vitality. She still had a long way to go, but she was well enough to be left by herself.

"Rick and I are going to see Dr. Shepherd," he told her. "He wants to put us in the hospital. Will you be alright here alone?"

"Sure," she replied. "I'll be fine, and if something comes up, I'll know where to find you."

"Yeah," Nick agreed. "Rick phoned the doctor yesterday and he thought we might do okay at Dodge Memorial. It's a private hospital and the doc thinks they can do us some good. They're set up to handle drug problems, so that's where we're going." Grinning broadly, he added, "Maybe it'll give the cops a different slant on us. At least they'll know we're not breaking any laws while we're in there."

WALKING A CROOKED PATH

"Crimes are not to be measured by the issue of events, but from the bad intentions of men."
Marcus Tullius Cicero
(106 - 43 B.C.)

Dodge Memorial Hospital was the epitome of medical care. It was located on the banks of the Miami River with rolling lawns and tall palms. A private hospital, it catered to the monied crowd and specialized in personal problems related to all kinds of addictions and mental disorders. Both Nick and Rick could well afford the treatment they were seeking, but their habits proved greater than their desire to be clean. Heroin's grip on them was too strong and their resolution was too weak.

It was only a matter of days before Nick asked Gretchen to bring him a fix. Rick's arrangements for himself were provided by a secret stash he had brought in with him. This is how they defeated themselves, and even after her terrible ordeal getting off the stuff, Gretchen returned to the needle and joined them in their downfall.

Coming out of the hospital still addicted to heroin, Nick was forced to find a new and ongoing means of maintaining their habits. The money they needed was no longer rolling in and their reserve capital was disappearing fast. Gretchen's jewelry was the first to go, but it wasn't enough. There was no end to their need for heroin. Every day held a new battle demanding their surrender.

As a confirmed and committed addict, Nick discovered that many of his old connections and so-called friends no longer trusted him. They were still polite, but they knew he wasn't in control of his actions. He was a junkie and they knew he'd do anything to anyone to get the dope he needed. Where his word had once been his bond, it was now worthless in a business sense. Direct participation in crimes of a different sort was the only avenue left open to him. Nick gave himself over to violence with a drug-filled passion that drove him from one excess to another.

He knew his way around the drug circle. Nick was well aware of who was selling, and his reputation in the bars and clubs was well known. People were constantly coming to him for the dope they wanted to buy. These people were not dealers. They were users, looking for a fix. Nick would agree to make a buy for them, knowing they would give him the cash in advance.

"Look," he'd tell them, "we'll drive your car over to this bar I know. I'll go inside and make the score and bring it out to you."

If the buyers agreed to his terms, he'd have them drive into a very seedy neighborhood where he knew they wouldn't want to get out of the car, take their money and let them wait. There was never a lot of money involved, maybe $100 or less, but enough to make the score he needed for himself. With his so-called customer trusting him, he'd make the connection and wander out through the back door. This generally led to a *shooting gallery* where everyone was shooting up and getting high. On his way out, he'd spot somebody who needed a hit and proposition him.

"Man," he'd tell him, "I just scored some dope and I'll split it with you if you'll do me a little favor."

It was very seldom that such a proposition was

rejected and Nick would explain, "After we shoot-up, I want you to run out the front door and take off down the street. I'll give you a minute and then I'll come out and chase you around the corner."

"Is that all you want me to do?"

"Yeah," Nick would admit with a sly look in his eyes.

They would go through the routine, and after making it look good for the guy waiting in the car, Nick would come back, looking angry and disgusted, to report, "That guy ripped me off! He's got your money and I couldn't catch him. If you want to come with me, I'll keep looking, but it really isn't safe wandering around these old buildings."

The customer would generally say, "Naw, forget it." They rarely offered to give Nick a ride back to where they picked him up, but he was always feeling high by then, and didn't mind taking a taxi with some of their money.

Nick continued this practice until the word got around and people stopped coming to him for dope. It was the beginning of his scramble for the daily drug needs he and Gretchen continued to face. Every morning, he knew they had to make a score or suffer.

With this need constantly pushing them, Nick and Gretchen became thieves. She would steal her mother's check book and forge her signature for the cash they needed to buy dope. They also started stealing her mother's valuable antiques. They would haul them down to *antique row* and peddle them for whatever they could get, then make a connection and shoot-up before returning home. Her mother made good on the checks and she missed the things they stole, but she put up with it and continued praying for the two of them.

These prayers were answered in a way that neither Gretchen nor her mother expected. As heroin increased its daily demands on Nick and

Gretchen, more checks were written and cashed. Almost every day, the bank would call Mrs. Martz to learn if she would continue making them good. Eventually, she was forced to call Gretchen to account.

"This check writing has to stop." Madeleine declared firmly. "I can't cover for you any longer. You and Nick have been stealing from me for months, and if it happens one more time, I'm going to call the police!"

"Mother," Gretchen pleaded, "I feel terrible about this, but we were in pain. I was helpless to do anything else."

"That's not true," he mother responded. "You both could stop using drugs and then Nick could hold a job again. The radio station would take him back if they could depend on him to show up and do the job."

"You don't understand," Gretchen insisted. "We have tried to stop and it almost killed us."

"Listen to me, young lady," Madeleine stated, "there are programs to help you, and if you don't get into one right now, I'll let them come and get you. You need help, and a little prayer wouldn't hurt. You'd have to quit *cold-turkey* if you were in jail."

Jail-time was something Gretchen really feared. She'd heard stories of how female inmates were treated by the other inmates. She wasn't physically strong enough to fight for her virtue and the prospect of being raped by a lesbian *butch* terrified her.

"Okay, mother," she reluctantly agreed, "I'll get into another program, but I really don't think it'll do any good."

Later that day, when Gretchen reported her mother's ultimatum to Nick, his reaction came as no surprise. He suggested that she check out the various drug programs and select one that would satisfy her mother.

"In the meantime," he stated, "I think I have a different solution to our problem." Smiling confidently, he added, "There's a lot of money around that can be ours for the taking."

"Go on," Gretchen urged.

"I've got a few things lined up that'll take care of us for awhile and you won't have to be involved. You can go along with your mother's idea and keep her off our backs while I get us on track with a little breaking and entering."

"What happens if you get caught?" Gretchen asked.

Nick laughed before he answered. "The jobs I've got in mind won't even be reported to the police."

"Why not?"

"I'm going to steal the kind of stuff the owners don't want to admit they had in the first place," he replied, "the kind of money and stuff they can't explain without setting themselves up for a bust." Grinning with delight, he revealed a couple of examples of what he had in mind.

"There's a heroin deal coming down in the next few days that'll be easy picking off. I've got a couple of guys standing by and we'll hit 'em for either the money or the dope. The man making the deal works out of his home, so we'll go in when he's alone and rip him off."

"Won't he come after you?" Gretchen asked.

"Don't worry, honey," Nick chortled, "when I get through with him, I'll be the last guy in the world he'll ever want to see again. We'll either have his heroin or the ten grand he made by selling it."

"What's going to happen to us while we wait for this deal to come down?" Gretchen pressed.

"I've got that figured, too," Nick answered. "Remmember when we were working at Eddie's Adult Book Store?" Gretchen nodded and he continued, "Well, Eddie has that girl of his go around to all his stores every Tuesday and collect the money from his movie machines." He grinned again. "She does this late in the day and takes her collection home in a briefcase that she leaves in the locked trunk of her car. It's all in rolls of quarters and too heavy for her to carry upstairs to her apartment.

"I'm going to have Kathy drive me out to her place tonight. We'll wait until she gets home and goes to sleep, then I'll break into her car and get the briefcase. We should get over a thousand dollars for just a few minutes work."

Kathy was a few years older than Gretchen and Nick felt she would be more levelheaded on a job that involved actual participation, so he phoned her. She agreed to go along on the deal and promised to pick him up a little after midnight.

They drove out to the girl's apartment, parked the car a couple of doors down the street and waited. It was almost 3:30 in the morning before she arrived in her Oldsmobile Toronado. They watched her get out and lock the car.

"We'll wait until she's in bed and asleep," Nick whispered. "Then I'll slip a wire down inside the car and pull the lock. These Toronados have a button in the glove compartment that pops the trunk. After I check the briefcase, I'll signal you to pull up to me. I'll throw the briefcase in the back of your car and we'll take off."

"She probably won't know the money's gone," Kathy smirked, "until she goes to the bank in the morning."

"Yeah," Nick agreed. "This is like taking candy from a baby. We'll be out of here in less than five minutes."

They watched the lights in the girl's apartment go out, then waited another 30 minutes before Nick slipped out of Kathy's car and walked over to the Oldsmobile. It took him about a minute to unlock the door and pop the trunk lid. He opened the briefcase and chuckled softly. It was jammed with rolls of quarters, so full the lid bulged as he closed the bag and snapped the hasp.

Turning toward Kathy's car, he signaled for her to pull up alongside the Olds. She rolled her back window down for him to toss the bag into the car as she approached slowly. She wouldn't have to stop because he could get in beside her as the car was rolling.

As she started toward him, Nick picked up the bag. It was very heavy and he knew he'd have to swing it with all his strength, but when he started his swing, the bag popped open and rolls of quarters suddenly flew through the air in every direction. Several of the rolls broke open as they hit the pavement. In the early morning stillness, it sounded like the loudest church chimes in the world.

There were quarters all over the street, rolling and jingling like a circus calliope. Nick nervously peered up and down the street. He was positive the noise would awaken everyone and attract unwanted attention. Kathy stopped the car. She couldn't understand what had happened, but when she saw Nick scrambling around scooping quarters back into the briefcase, she joined him.

They were both ready to bolt at the first sign of discovery. Kathy had left the car running for a quick getaway, but no one seemed to respond to all the noise, so they continued gathering the quarters. It took them 30 minutes to refill the briefcase, but they got every quarter before climbing into the car and leaving.

Once they were under way, Kathy started giggling. As first Nick was slightly irritated by her laughter, but as he thought about how they must have looked, crawling around on the pavement, throwing quarters back into the bag, he started laughing as well.

"Damn!" he snorted with laughter, "I'm surprised the police didn't hear all that jingling all the way down town."

"Yeah," Kathy chortled, "we would have made a fine picture on our hands and knees, picking up quarters in the dark."

"It's a good thing Eddie's girl is a sound sleeper," Nick commented. "If she'd just looked out her bedroom window, or turned on her bedroom light, we'd have left the quarters for her to pick up."

"What's next?" Kathy asked.

"We'll go get Gretchen," Nick said, "then I'll buy us some dope and we'll go to a motel and get off. I think we deserve a little reward for our night's work. Don't you agree?"

"Right on!" Kathy responded.

"After checking into the motel and getting off, Nick paid Kathy off with a $100 piece of heroin and she left. He dumped the remaining rolls of quarters out on the bed for Gretchen to count as he told her what had happened. She also giggled as he described how he and Kathy had scrambled to get the money back in the bag, but the *quarter rip-off,* as they eventually called it, produced enough money to keep their needs satisfied for almost a week while they waited for the other deal to come down.

Nick arranged for two friends to join him on this job. He planned to forcibly enter the man's home when he answered their knock and Nick didn't want to be surprised if there were others in the house. He wasn't expecting too much trouble, but he wanted to be covered for any contingency, and this required three men inside the house. There was also another factor to be considered.

This was going to come down as an armed robbery, and he needed someone to drive and stay with the car. Since he didn't want to split the take four ways, he asked Gretchen to do the driving. Nick

131

didn't like the idea of involving Gretchen, but she had driven for him on a few other occasions and this time, if the police got involved, she could easily drive away without anyone suspecting she was with them. After Nick explained, Gretchen agreed to go along on the job.

"Honey," he told her, "we won't be inside more than fifteen minutes. I'll stick my gun in the man's face and make him tell me where he's hidden the money. Harry will keep watch to warn us if anyone else comes toward the house. Joe will tie the man up and keep him covered while I get the money. You can stay in the car with the lights out and the engine running. The whole deal won't take more than thirty minutes and we'll have $10,000 for our trouble."

"Are you sure the man will be alone when you go in?" she questioned.

"He lives alone," Nick answered, "but he might have somebody with him. That's why I'm not pulling this off by myself."

"Are you sure he'll have the money in the house?"

"He'll either have the money or the dope," he said with a grin, "and I really don't care which it is. One's just as good as the other."

Nodding her head in agreement, Gretchen asked, "When do we do it?"

"Tonight," he declared. "Harry and Joe will meet us here at ten o'clock. It'll take us about 30 minutes to drive over to the guy's place and we should be back here before midnight."

The man lived in a very nice section of the city, featuring sweeping front lawns that were well land-scaped with wide open areas between all the sur-rounding homes. Gretchen parked the car at the curb in front of the house, turned off the headlights and watched the three men walk up to the front door. She expected them to finish the job fast and return to

132

the car with very little trouble. Nick and his two companions had expressed great confidence in the plan during the ride across town.

Standing on the front steps, Nick motioned the other two to stand aside, out of sight, as he rang the doorbell. There were lights on in the house, so he knew the man hadn't gone to bed. With his gun in hand, he waited for his ring to be answered. As the man opened the door cautiously, Nick jammed his shoulder against it, shoving the door open and his victim back into the entry hallway.

"Narcotics! Police!" Nick yelled. "Get on the floor!"

In complete panic, the man immediately, dropped to the floor on his face with his arms and legs spread. Keeping him covered, Nick motioned Joe into the house. They'd been informed the man would be alone and unarmed, but Nick wanted to be sure before they started working the guy over for the money.

Harry stayed with Nick as Joe proceeded to search the house. In a couple of minutes, Joe returned with a man he'd found upstairs. Grinning widely, he said, "This guy was charging down the upstairs hallway with a gun in his hand. He was as surprised to see me as I was to see him, but when I told him he was under arrest, he gave me his gun and dropped to the floor."

Turning to Harry, Nick snapped, "Get these two guys tied up! Pull the extension cords off of those floor lamps and tie 'em good."

Both men were tied to a couple of dining room chairs when Nick demanded, "Okay, we know you've just worked a cocaine deal and you've got ten grand here in the house. We want that money, and we want it now."

"Look, man," the guy whined, "I put that money in my safety deposit box earlier today. There's no money in this house."

"Don't give me that crap!" Nick roared. "You'd better come up with the cash, or I'm going to make you wish you had!" Grabbing the man's collar, Nick viciously backhanded him across the face and yelled, "Where is it?"

"Honest," the man whimpered, "I haven't got it. It's in the bank."

Driving his fist into the man's stomach, Nick snarled, "If you don't have the money, then you've still got the dope!" Hitting him again, Nick hissed, "I'll take the dope, but we're not leaving here without everything you've got! Give it up now! If you don't, you're going to be hurt bad!"

"Well, I haven't got anything to give you," the man insisted.

"I'll break your nose," Nick growled, "and we'll see what you say then." Slamming his fist into the man's face, Harry and Joe heard the crushing impact of the blow as the man screamed in pain. "Where is it? Tell me now or I'll beat you to death!"

"Please," the man pleaded, "believe me, the dope is gone and the money isn't here."

"I think he's telling the truth," Joe shouted.

"Let's search the house," Harry suggested. "It should be easy to find, and if he's telling the truth it won't do any good to kill him."

"Okay," Nick agreed. "You guys stay here and watch these two. I'll look around and see what I can find."

Leaving them in the dining room, he started a systematic search of every room on the ground floor before moving on to the upstairs. As Nick entered one of the bedrooms, he found another man sleeping. Placing the barrel of his gun against the man's head, Nick woke him with a roar. "Get out of that bed!"

The man had been sleeping in his shorts, so Nick marched him downstairs dressed that way. He wasn't sure who belonged in the house, and since the first man hadn't told him anything, Nick started working on the new man, letting the other two see what he was doing. They all remained silent and Nick blew his cool.

Striding across the room to the glass-fronted china cabinet, he pulled it away from the wall and tipped it over, sending broken glass and china all over the floor. Grabbing the man by his hair, Nick jammed his gun and fist into the man's stomach.

"I'm only going to ask one more time, and if I don't get the answer I want, you're going to bleed a lot of blood! Now, where is the ten thousand dollars?"

"We haven't got that kind of money here," the man responded in fear. "I don't know what you're talking about."

Nick slapped him on the side of his head with the gun, knocking him to his knees. Kicking him in the chest, Nick forced him over on his back. The man was screaming with pain as Nick started dragging him through the broken glass, leaving a trail of blood in his wake. After the man's back and chest had been turned into a raw mass of bleeding flesh, he passed out and Nick dropped him to the floor.

"I don't think they've got anything here," Joe volunteered. "If they did, they would have certainly told us by now."

"Yeah," Harry agreed, "let's get out of here! This deal is a bust."

Kicking each man in the groin, Nick finally agreed. They'd torn up the house, wrecked the dining room and crippled their victims, so with anger and frustration in his heart, Nick led Harry and Joe from the house.

As they drove back across town, Gretchen asked, "What happened?"

"It wasn't there," Nick answered sourly. "That sucker had put the money in his safety deposit box after selling the cocaine."

"What was all the screaming about?" she pressed

"I had to question them, and when they wouldn't

135

tell me where the money was hidden, I worked them over."

"Nick," she said, "I thought you were wrecking the place. I was about to drive off, knowing you were making so much noise that it was only a matter of time before the neighbors called the police."

"I know," Nick admitted bitterly, "it was supposed to be a fast, simple hiest, and I'm surprised the police didn't come. We were in there too long, but I didn't want to admit that I'd made a mistake."

A friend with Nick during heroin days.

MISTAKES COME EASIER

*"Experience is the name everyone
gives to his mistakes."*

Oscar Wilde
(1856 - 1900)

Gretchen and Nick were forced to recognize the growing pressure of their habits. Her heroin needs had reached $400 per day while his had peaked at $800. This meant they now had to raise $8,400 per week for a yearly total of $436,800. In facing this level of addiction, they had little choice in what they could do. The only way they could raise this kind of money was through crime—not merely small time crime, but the demanding type that never quits. They needed almost half a million dollars just for dope in a year's time, and when they accepted this fact, they knew their lives were being controlled by the master neither of them wanted to acknowledge. Heroin was the master of their bodies, souls, and minds. The ape on their backs had become a full-grown, insatiable gorilla.

Under pressure of this kind, there were many days when they didn't achieve their heroin-dictated goal and they paid the price with the agony of denial. Nerves stretched to the breaking point, Gretchen and Nick started taking risks they would have avoided only a few months earlier. Every waking hour was dominated by the demands of their addiction. Immediately after getting a fix, they began thinking and planning for the next one because they knew they weren't strong enough to escape the vice-like grip of their chemical master.

The plight of Gretchen and Nick clearly illustrates the single most critical problem facing the nation today. It has been estimated there are 500,000 hard-core heroin addicts in the United States. If they have an average of $100 per day addiction, the daily heroin market calls for the expenditure of $50 million. 99% of this is generated through crime. In a year's time, the total comes to over $18 billion, much of it supplied by unwilling victims through crimes against the public.

Add the addiction of an estimated 3 million cocaine addicts and it's extremely easy to understand why our prisons are overloaded with drug-related criminals. Crimes resulting from drug traffic are not limited to suppliers, dealers and pushers. Users, to support their habits, commit the majority of the crimes, and the people of America are the primary victims. Cocaine addiction, in addition to being expensive to the tune of over $20 billion every year, is responsible for a great deal of white collar crime.

On the average, it takes about $18,000 to keep one person in prison for a year. This charge must be added to our law enforcement expenditure. It isn't difficult to understand how the so-called drug culture is draining the nation's strength. Directly and indirectly the people of the United States are paying well over $100 billion dollars annually in a losing fight that involves marijuana, cocaine, speed, crack, heroin, and all the other current favorites.

Added to the tragedy of all this is the fact that drug addiction is becoming more and more common among the young people who hold the greatest promise for the future. It isn't uncommon to find children under the age of 12 hooked on the needle. This is particularly true in the lower income neighborhoods of our larger cities where the drug dealer and pusher have become role-models for the kids. They dress well, drive big cars, spend money lavishly and create the impression of great personal success and power. The kids, full of admiration for these people, seldom see them when they fall victim to the poison they've been spreading. Gretchen and Nick are prime examples of the great drug fallacy.

Nick was no longer the glamorous radio voice introducing the music they liked to hear. The big cars were gone and the seemingly endless stream of $100 bills had stopped flowing into Gretchen's boxes and bags. They had become thieves, armed robbers and muggers. They no longer wanted to be seen doing their *thing*.

After months of scrambling for, and not always meeting, their daily needs, Nick and Gretchen moved back to Madeleine's. This was dictated by their need to make every dollar go as far as possible. It wasn't a happy time for them and Nick knew they needed to make a big score, something to maintain them for more than a few days. Need made him ready to take greater chances.

Coming home with enough heroin for a couple of days, Nick eagerly told Gretchen, "There's a deal cooking that'll get us back on our feet. I ran into the *Iron Man* this afternoon and he wanted to know if I could still handle a fairly large shipment of heroin. I told him we'd take all he could give us."

"Is he on the level?" Gretchen asked.

"Yeah," Nick replied. "He's hooked up with *Cho Cho* Cleare and a couple of other guys and they're set up over at the Ramada Inn in Hallandale. They want me to reopen my old pipeline and take the stuff they're bringing in."

"How big is it?" she pressed. "Can we depend on them to keep us supplied when we get started again?"

"I think so," he said with a grin. "They've got 250

grand worth of heroin on hand right now and they've started to cut it for the street. They want us to come over and check it out. I told them we'd be there right after Thanksgiving dinner with your mother."

"Then you want me to go with you?" Gretchen questioned.

"Yes," he answered, "they know what I've been doing for the past few months and they also know the cops are paying extra attention to my activities. They figure if you're with me, I won't be setting them up to make the police go easier on me."

"The *Iron Man* knows you'd never blow the whistle on a deal," she remarked, "but if it'll make his friends relax a little by having me around, so be it."

This was in November of 1974. Gretchen was now 20 and Nick was 31. They were tired of the struggle and ready to seize any deal promising even a modicum of peace. Nick was uncomfortably aware that the police always seemed to be nearby. Every time he looked out an apartment window, he saw a police car slowly cruising past, often another one was parked a little way down the street. Nothing overt happened. It was as if they were just waiting for him to make a mistake before coming down on him. Gretchen also noticed more police attention to her activities, but her limited involvement kept her from being too concerned.

While driving over to the Ramada Inn, Nick took special pains to make sure they weren't followed. He doubled back several times, checking all the cars in his rearview mirror to be certain the police weren't using more than one car. He was totally unaware that the Broward County Sheriff, Edward Stack, already had secret agents watching the activities taking place at the motel. He and Gretchen walked into this trap just a few hours before the sheriff's agents raided the operation.

They were arrested along with four others and

charged with the possession of narcotic paraphernalia and heroin. The same charge was filed against *Iron Man,* and bail was set at $12,500 each. Ralph Deffenbaugh was charged with delivery of heroin, possession of heroin and possession of narcotic paraphernalia. His bail was set at $37,500.

George *Cho Cho* Cleare, in whose name the room was registered, was charged with two counts of delivery of heroin, one count of possession of heroin, possession of paraphernalia and possession of a firearm during the commission of a felony. He was held on a $64,000 bond.

David Robinson was charged with three counts of delivery of heroin and one count of possession. His bond was set at $85,000. George Barr, an associate of *Iron Man,* was charged with possession of marijuana, heroin, and paraphernalia. His bond was set at $13,000.

For Gretchen, this was the occasion of two unwanted "firsts": her first newspaper headline, and her first arrest. Going through the booking process, she was fingerprinted, photographed and placed in a holding cell. The story continued to be news, extending the humiliation of her arrest, because it involved a jurisdictional dispute between the sheriff's office and the Hallandale police. In the end, however, the authorities were forced to release everyone except *Cho Cho.* It was his room at the motel. The others were merely his guests. The sheriff's officers alleged that he was operating a drug "factory" at the motel and preparing to distribute street-quality heroin from that location.

Gretchen spent eight days behind bars. Her fear of incarceration never left her and she felt intimidated whenever she came into contact with any of the other female prisoners. She was terrified, but a family friend who was a juvenile probation officer "wined and dined" a judge and got her released. Until the charges were dismissed, Gretchen was free in the custody of Madeleine's friend while Nick and the others remained in jail.

Gretchen's eight days served another purpose, however, as she was forced to go *cold-turkey* for the entire time. This opened her eyes to what she was doing to herself. She was overwhelmed by feelings of guilt and disappointment at what she had done with her life. The day she was released, she firmly resolved to change her lifestyle and regain her sense of pride. This was the answer to Madeleine's prayers. God had finally gotten Gretchen's attention.

The sheriff's case was further weakened by a strange foul-up with the evidence they had seized during the arrest. The heroin they captured had been pure white, but when they went to the police property room to get it for testing, a brown substance had replaced it. Someone with official access to the property room had stolen the pure. The authorities were therefore unable to prove that heroin had ever been seized. This in turn, made the heroin charges against everyone involved seem ludicrous, leaving only the paraphernalia and firearm charges to be resolved. Since the felony charges couldn't be proven, these charges became meaningless.

Ironically, Hallandale's Police Chief, James Longo, was attending a dinner in his honor at the same motel while the sheriff's officers were conducting the raid. Longo was being honored by the Hallandale High School for his efforts in crime prevention among the school's students. He didn't learn of the narcotic arrests until he was contacted by newspaper reporters the following day.

As the jurisdictional squabble continued between the sheriff and the police chief, the arrest that brought it to a head seemed to diminish in importance. Eventually the newspapers carried stories of the law enforcement conflict without mentioning the Ramada

142

affair, and when Nick was released the arrest was completely forgotten.

While awaiting Nick's return, Gretchen became involved in a drug program located in West Palm Beach. Within a few days, she came under heavy conviction by the Holy Spirit. This was the format the program was following and it gave Gretchen a new fear. This fear helped her see how rotten she'd become, and the sins she'd committed weighed heavily on her mind. She couldn't take it, and ran away from the program, but the guilt she felt didn't disappear.

Arriving home in Fort Lauderdale during an electrical storm, she was entering the apartment when lightning struck three palm trees in the yard. Convinced that God had directed the lightning to punish her, Gretchen ran inside and huddled in the middle of the livng room floor. She was terrified, and certain God's anger was directed at her.

This conviction did not leave her, and when Nick finally arrived, she met him with firm resolve. He was totally unprepared for her change in attitude as he stood framed in the doorway and faced her.

"Hi, honey," he shouted joyfully, "they dropped all their charges and I'm free as a bird." Stepping into the living room, he added, "I scored some good dope on the way home. Let's get off together."

Gretchen opened her mouth to speak, not knowing what she was going to say, and the words just came tumbling out. "Are you crazy? The wrath of God is upon me and I'm going to hell!"

"What are you talking about?" Nick demanded. "Have you lost your mind? What's this about the wrath of...." He stopped talking. Her eyes were blazing with an emotion he hadn't seen before.

"I told you I'm going to hell," she snapped. "God is going to punish me for all the sins I've committed!"

Something told Nick not to press the question

any further. It was obvious something had happened and until he understood what it was, he should remain silent. Taking Gretchen in his arms, he tried to erase her negative attitude with a show of affection, but she didn't respond to his embrace. Without saying another word, he released her and went into the bathroom, feeling he'd be better able to face her rejection after getting off himself. He could almost feel her cold silence as he closed the bathroom door.

For the balance of the day, and that night, Gretchen maintained a stony silence and icy reserve. She didn't try to explain her actions and Nick didn't attempt to force an explanation from her. It was as if they'd called a truce in their relationship.

It isn't like her, he thought while drifting off to sleep, *to be like this. Someone, or something, has changed her. They must have done something to her while she was in jail.* Thinking she would explain everything in the morning, he slept beside her as if she weren't in the bed with him. He was confused and upset, but knew there was nothing he could do until she told him what was wrong.

Early the next morning, they were seated at the breakfast table drinking coffee when she grimly announced, "I've always known it was a sin to live with you the way I have all this time." Staring at him over the rim of her coffee cup, she firmly stated, "I love you, Nick, but we're no longer going to have sex and we're not going to continue living together!"

"Hey, wait a minute," Nick protested, slamming his fist down on the table. "You're my girl and I love you. We've been together too long to break everything off like this." Leaning toward her, he added, "I don't know what's happened to you, but our relationship is a two-way street and I'm not giving you up over some silly girlish notion that God is going to punish you for loving me!"

"He wants us both to change," she insisted.

144

"You're as guilty of sin as I am. We've got to get right with God or He's going to destroy us both!"

"No way!" Nick shouted, getting to his feet. "I'll give you time to think about all this, and I'll leave you alone while you do your thinking, but you're still my girl. Nobody's going to change that, not even God!"

"I want us both to get straight," Gretchen declared. "I'm going to move back into the house with Mother. You can stay here in the apartment, but until we're clean with God, I can't give you all the love I have in my heart."

Nick had to accept her decision, and in a strange way, he could understand her feelings. He was starting to feel disgusted with the life they were leading. He knew they had to change, but at that moment, he really didn't know what could be done to make the change they needed. Before he had a chance to think very much about it, his addiction dictated the terms of his immediate action. It was another day and his craving hadn't changed, so as far as he was concerned, the *rat race* still had to be run at least one more time.

As Gretchen started attending AA meetings and continued her outpatient involvement in another drug abuse program, Nick embarked on a crime wave to keep himself supplied with heroin. Gretchen still hadn't met Jesus in a personal way, but her fear of God was giving her the wisdom she needed to keep searching for the peace and understanding she so desperately needed.

Nick—Jail? A favor?

A COP DOES NICK A FAVOR

*"For though we may think we are specially blest,
We are certain to pay for the favors we get!"*

John Godfrey Saxe
(1816 - 1887)

Following Gretchen's lead, Nick began attending AA meetings. He hadn't come under the kind of conviction she felt, but he was rapidly becoming more and more tired of the treadmill of his life. The AA meetings, and the references to God, didn't stop any of his criminal activities, but a seed had been planted in his thoughts that he found difficult to ignore. He considered himself a junkie and continued to believe, "once a junkie, always a junkie," but the seed sprouted in the back of his brain, he began to hope for a drug-free life.

The other men at these meetings understood his problem. They tried to support him with their witness and their sympathy, still volunteering to face his withdrawal battle with him, even after he confessed there were arrest warrants out on him. At one meeting, several of them approached him with the same suggestion.

"Nick," they recommended, "you're never going to beat this thing without being honest with yourself. You should turn yourself in to the police. You've violated your probation, but that isn't the end of the world. Getting it straightened out is a good way to start on your road back to a full, rich life."

"You're all correct," Nick agreed. "The first thing Monday morning, I'll do it."

Monday came, but Nick didn't keep his promise. It was the same on Tuesday, Wednesday and Thursday. *Getting myself straight,* he rationalized, *is better than getting myself locked up. Maybe the answer I need is spiritual. I haven't been able to whip this thing on my own. Maybe a higher power is what I need.*

This was the core of Nick's problem. He didn't believe there was a higher power. The God he knew wasn't very nice, loving or understanding. Nick viewed God as a punishing, authority figure, and couldn't accept any other concept. The way the other men related to God didn't fit the God-image Nick had created in his mind. All of this thinking was conceived under the constant pressure of his heroin addiction. Heroin was the god he knew personally and he understood the demands this god made on his body and mind, but he was beginning to question his abject surrender to the chemical his body craved.

Do I really need to accept the fact that once a junkie, always a junkie? he asked himself. *Do I really need to live with that thought in my mind? When I die, will it be from an overdose with the needle still in my arm? Why do I need chemicals and drugs in my body when the guy next door doesn't? Why do I have to be high in order to enjoy food, sex or a movie? Other people enjoy these things naturally, why can't I?* His next question was the most important of all. *What's wrong with me?*

Nick knew the answers to these questions, but his craving for heroin wouldn't let him accept them. He had understood and accepted Gretchen's expressed need for change, but the *gorilla* on his back prevented him from applying that need to himself. Nick hadn't come under the conviction of the Holy Spirit as she had, and that was the Rubicon he still had to cross.

His mind was filled with need, but the *gorilla* kept telling him, "All you need is money and dope."

As he considered the important part God played in the 12 steps of the AA program, Nick began to wonder if God had ever taken an active interest in his life. His Roman Catholic background hadn't prepared him for this consideration, but he couldn't help thinking of what God might have done to save him from himself. As these thoughts mushed through his subconscious, Nick began remembering incidents that had made no sense to him at the time of their occurrence. He didn't realize God was gently reminding him of times he would have utterly destroyed his life if something unnatural hadn't been done to stop him, like the time he and his friend, Willie, had spent an afternnoon getting high in Willie's hotel room. They'd both gotten off with the same needle and as the heroin spun its web over Nick's brain, he laid his revolver on the table, then leaned back in the chair and closed his eyes. Willie picked up the gun, commenting on its weight and feel.

"It's a beauty," Willie said, "but I prefer a .32 automatic. They're not as heavy as your .38 police special."

Nick didn't bother to open his eyes as he responded, "My dad carries a .38 police special, and if it's good enough for him, it's good enough for me. Besides, I like its hitting power." Opening his eyes, Nick heaved himself out of the chair and headed for the bathroom. He didn't see Willie unload the .38 and put the rounds safely into the dresser drawer. Willie had no idea Nick was planning to rob a bank messenger later that evening and he forgot to tell Nick that he'd unloaded the gun.

One of Nick's cardinal rules was *never go out to do a job with an unloaded gun*. In his opinion, if a gun was unloaded, it was useless and should be left at home. As their conversation drifted on to other subjects, the gun was forgotten until it was time for Nick's rendezvous with the messenger.

Nick was wearing a sport shirt and slacks, and as he prepared to leave Willie's room, he slipped his piece inside his waistband, letting the shirt hang out to conceal the weapon. He knew where he was going and what he was going to do and the gun was an important part of his plan. He'd cased the job for almost a week and knew the messenger's routine.

After picking up the night deposits from three liquor stores, the man always parked his car at the entrance to an alley next to the bank. Nick planned to hit him in the alley as he walked from his car to the night deposit slot on the corner. Waiting out of sight, he watched the man pull up and get out of the car before approaching him silently from the back.

Grabbing the man's free arm, Nick jammed it up into the small of his back with one hand while pulling out his piece with the other. He automatically cocked the revolver as he drew it from his waistband and jammed it against the man's head, right behind his ear. Nick's thumb accidently slipped, letting the hammer fall, and he froze, expecting to see the man's head explode into a bloody mush. When nothing happened, he figured the gun had misfired and cocked it again before slugging the man with it and grabbing his deposit bag.

The messenger went down without a sound and Nick walked up the alley to his car and left the scene. He was shaking slightly as he considered what might have happened. It had never been his intention to kill the messenger, but the fact that his gun hadn't fired startled him. It was a snub-nosed Smith & Wesson, not a *Saturday-night special,* and he couldn't understand why it had failed to fire.

As these thoughts roared through his head, Nick suddenly realized that he could have killed the man. This would have added murder to his string of crimes and that was a charge he didn't want on his record. There's no statute of limitations on murder, and if the gun had fired, the murder would have hung over him for the rest of his life. Nothing could have saved him from that never-ending charge.

As he looked back on the incident, following an AA meeting, Nick suddenly became convinced that God had taken a hand in the affair by letting Willie unload his piece. There was no reason for Willie to do what he did. He'd never done it before, and the fact that he hadn't told Nick about it as he left the room seemed to confirm that God just might have something He wanted Nick to do for Him. This possibility stayed in Nick's mind and triggered other memories.

He remembered how he and Gretchen, while working in the adult book store had often used the water from the bathroom commode to prepare their heroin needles. He's been aware of the danger of infection, but something, or Someone, had always managed to keep them both clean. There were also times he'd borrowed used needles in some of the filthiest of shooting galleries and come away clean. As memories like these crowded his mind, Nick's awareness of God started to grow in his brain. He was still enslaved to heroin and compelled to obey the demands of his body, but his brain was entering a phase of thinking that hadn't occurred before. For the first time, he was able to accept the existence of God and relate Him to some of the events in his life.

Although they were no longer living together, Gretchen and Nick were still seeing each other and she knew what he was into. She was finally breaking her habit, with the firm conviction of the Holy Spirit, and was encouraged by the changes she saw growing in Nick.

He was still hooked and maintaining his habit through breaking and entering and other crimes, but she could see that he was not the same Nick she'd known for so long. Gretchen showed her concern for his spiritual growth by keeping tabs on his activities and praying for his safety. There was nothing she could do to change his activities, but she was learning to be patient with his rebellious attitude. Nick showed no concern for himself because he still believed he was able to take care of his needs regardless of the chances he was taking. He and Willie soon learned the fallacy of this belief.

They both needed money for drugs, and after reading the society pages of the newspaper to learn who might be away on holiday or hosting a party on their yacht, they planned a little breaking and entering. A news item about a farewell party for a couple leaving for Europe caught their attention. The home was in a very affluent neighborhood along one of the canals in Ft. Lauderdale. The people would be away for three weeks, so what was stolen wouldn't be reported until after it was sold and the money spent. At 11:00 o'clock that night, they drove over in Willie's car, parking it in the shadows out of sight.

They entered the house from the rear, crossing the garden terrace and breaking a pane of glass in the French doors. Working as a team, they went from room to room, selecting what they wanted and piling the loot on the kitchen floor where it could easily be transferred to the car later. As they entered each room, they turned on the lights for a quick inspection of its contents, turning them off as they finished. A neighbor, knowing the owners were away, noticed the lights and called the police.

While dumping the family silver in a pillow case, Nick glanced out the dining room window. A police car was stopping in the driveway. Hitting the light switch, he growled, "Willie, it's the cops! Follow me!"

The front of the house was blocked. They couldn't get to their car. Charging out through the French doors, they raced across the lawn to the boat dock on

152

the canal as the police entered the house. Slipping into the water, Nick and Willie swam under the dock without making a sound. With just their heads showing above water, they held their breath and waited.

"They must have gone into the canal," one of the officers shouted, throwing the beam of his flashlight out over the water.

"If their heads come up," another officer yelled, "just shoot 'em!"

Willie didn't like the water and his voice was tinged with panic as he whispered, "They're looking for us further out in the canal. I'm going to slip along next to the seawall and get out of here."

"You'll never make it," Nick whispered back. "The cops are standing on the seawall. They'll spot you for sure."

"They'll never see me in the dark," Willie muttered softly, making his way out from under the protective deck. He hadn't gone ten feet before his upturned face was framed in the beam of the cop's flashlight.

"Here's one of 'em," the man reported loudly. "Come and help me pull him out."

Nick remained hidden as they pulled Willie up onto the lawn. It was cold in the water and he was beginning to shiver, but he didn't make a move or a sound as they started questioning Willie.

"Where's your partner? Did he swim across the canal? Come on, tell us where he is."

Willie gave them no answers, but Nick's heart dropped when he saw and heard the approaching police boat with its big spotlight sweeping the water. It was only a matter of minutes before that bright beam of light was directed full in Nick's face.

"There's one under the dock," a cop on the boat yelled.

Nick heard heavy footsteps on the deck directly over his head as a deep voice ordered, "Okay, buster, come on out!"

Dripping wet, he was pulled up onto the dock, cuffed, read his rights, and arrested for breaking and entering. As he was marched into the police station, still wet and shivering with cold, Nick knew he couldn't make bail. With his previous record of arrests and jail time, his bail would be higher than Willie's, so he prepared himself for another extended period of county hospitality. It would mean going *cold turkey* again, but this time he felt better prepared by what he'd learned at the AA meetings.

Throughout his first court appearance the following morning, he was sick with his craving, but he managed to get through it. The date of his trial was set and it meant he'd spend the next six months in jail before it appeared on the court calendar. In six months time, Nick knew he'd be in better physical shape to face any challenge, and in any event, there was nothing he could do to shorten the time.

Gretchen was with her mother and deeply involved in completely conquering her addition, so he didn't have to worry about her. *At least,* he thought, *she can kick her habit in the free world while I kick mine in a jail cell.*

When his trial date finally rolled around, Nick was ready. He ran the whole game on the judge, admitting he needed help and begging for another break in justice. The judge reviewed his record and called a recess in the proceedings to allow time for Nick to be interviewed by the *Spectrum* people who were present in the courtroom.

Following the interview, and upon receiving the *Spectrum House* approval, Judge Daniel Futch sentenced Nick to "time-served" and six months probation and observation at the Ft. Lauderdale *Spectrum* facility. Nick was returned to his cell to pack his things and get ready to move out with his *Spectrum* escort. He was extremely pleased with the outcome of his trial, and as he gathered his stuff together, he bragged to his fellow inmates, "By eight o'clock tonight, I'll have a needle in my arm and blood stains on my shirt."

Arriving at the Ft. Lauderdale *Spectrum House,* Nick was told to sit on a bench in the reception room and wait to be called for processing. He had the box of his belongings with him. As he waited, he started to rearrange its contents. Suddenly, a man appeared in the doorway and ordered, "Don't touch that stuff!"

"Hey, it's mine," Nick retorted. "What do you mean?"

"Just sit there, be quiet, and don't touch nothing!" the man snapped.

Picking up his box, Nick got to his feet and stated flatly, "You tell Tom, your director, that I said thanks for getting me out of jail." Moving toward the entrance door, "Tell him I'll see him later."

"Where do you think you're going?" the man snarled.

"I'm gone," Nick answered with amusement as he opened the door and left the house.

No attempt was made to stop him and Nick knew his leaving would be reported as a violation of his probation, but he didn't care. He'd conned the judge and he was free, that's all that mattered. About two blocks from the house, he used the phone at a convenience store to call Gretchen. While waiting for her to come and pick him up, he silently gloated over the way he was rubbing the whole affair in Judge Futch's face. Futch had the reputation of being a "hard" judge and Nick savored the way he'd made a fool of him.

Even with Gretchen trying to influence him away from heroin, Nick was on the street less than 24 hours before he'd hooked up with another friend to "pop" cars. Every morning, he and Eddie would steal a car and drive down to the beach where they'd scout the parking areas for loot. At the beach most people leave their purses, wallets, watches and other valuables locked in their cars while they're swimming or sunning themselves in the sand.

When items like these were left out on the car seats, it was simple matter to "pop" the car's door, grab what they wanted and move on to the next stop. After hitting five or six, they'd split the take, buy some dope and spend the rest of the day getting off. This worked well for about three months, but when the police began receiving an unusual number of "car-popping" reports, they increased their patrols of the beach area. It wasn't long before Nick and Eddie came to their official attention.

The road which was generally lined with parked cars ran down the grassy, high ground above the beach area. This road was intersected at various points by access streets, but if a car inadvertantly got off the beaten track, or the approved parking areas, it quickly became axle-deep in soft sand. This provided a degree of traffic control neither Nick nor Eddie had acknowledged when considering the possibility of police pursuit.

One warm, summer afternoon, with the loot from three "popped" cars on them, Nick was driving slowly down the main road while Eddie scanned the parked vehicles for their next "pop". Looking in the rearview mirror, he spotted a police car coming up fast behind them.

"It's the cops!" he exclaimed, jamming his foot down on the accelerator.

"Let's get out of here!" Eddie yelled as their car picked up speed.

As they approached the first intersecting roadway, doing about 70 miles per hour, a police cruiser pulled into the intersection, blocking the road. Nick started to slow down.

"No, Nick!" Eddie screamed. "Hit it! Go right

156

through it! Don't stop!" He was bouncing in the seat, yelling at the top of his voice, "Run the pig down! Kill him!"

Perhaps Nick was tired of the hassle and the running, or just maybe the living Lord Jesus was sitting in the back seat, but something or Someone told Nick that his running days were over. Feeling a deep sense of relief, he jammed his foot down on the brakes.

"What are you doing?" Eddie shouted. "Keep going! Don't stop! Have you lost your mind?"

"This is the end of it," Nick responded calmly.

"No way, man!" Eddie barked as the car skidded to a stop just a few feet from the police car. Opening his door, Eddie jumped out and started running across the open beach. Nick lowered his head and slumped down in the driver's seat as the officer approached, gun in hand.

"Out of the car," he ordered. "Put your hands on the hood and spread your legs."

After being searched for weapons, Nick was cuffed, read his rights and ordered into the cruiser's back seat. He was suddenly encased in the steel cage of a closed and locked police car while the officers chased after Eddie. With the car not running and closed tight in the bright summer sun, it got hot fast. Sweat was pouring off Nick when the officers returned and put Eddie in the other police vehicle, but even in the heat, Nick felt at peace with himself.

When the officer started the car and headed for the police station, Nick leaned forward and said, "Thanks, I think you've just done me a very great favor."

Glancing over his shoulder the policeman snorted, "Favor? You're not playing with a full deck. You've been arrested, man, and you're going to jail on charges of grand theft-auto, breaking and entering, resisting arrest and possession of stolen goods.

You're in big trouble, and if you call that a 'favor', you haven't got both oars in the water."

"You missed one," Nick chortled.

"One what?" the officer asked.

"Another charge against me."

"Hey, man," he said, looking back with a grin. "Tell me more."

"I've also violated my probation," Nick replied. "I think Judge Futch will be glad to see me again."

"Brother," the officer concluded seriously, "you've sure got a strange taste in favors."

Gretchen and Nick have changed from master heroin to Lord Jesus

THE AWAKENING

" A new heart also will I give you,
and a new spirit will I put within you."

Ezekiel 36:26

After booking Nick into the Hollywood jail, the desk sergeant called Nick's father and told him what had happened. This came as no real surprise to Mr. Barbetta. He'd known what his son was into for a long time and didn't want to be bothered with his arrest.

"I've expected something like this to happen," he told the sergeant. "Nick's never paid any attention to what I had to say in the past, so he'll just have to handle this on his own. I can't and don't want to help him."

Nick expected this reaction from his father. In fact, if the sergeant had asked, Nick would have refused to let him make the phone call. The one time Nick was released to the custody of his dad, five years earlier, an argument occurred in front of his mother. Mr. Barbetta, in anger, threatened Nick with a gun. His mother's protest was all that saved the situation. His father was the last person in the world Nick would look to for help.

Within a few hours of his arrest, Nick was transferred to the Broward County Jail for confinement until his hearing date was set. It was here, over the next few days, that he finally kicked his habit. This was accomplished with the help of his earlier AA training and some AA books he found to read. While his body continued to cry out for heroin, Nick was able to find the strength he needed to win the fight. Recalling those desperate moments, he said, "It was a mystical kind of strength, and I vaguely remember feeling the 'higher power' that was so often mentioned at the AA meetings."

With sober thought, Nick was coming to an awareness of God. He found an old, dogeared Bible on the shelf in his cell and started reading Holy Scripture. The Book of Genesis confused him, and after four days of reading, he gave up and snapped it closed. The noise of the book closing attracted the attention of the man in the next cell. He was a backslidden Christian from Virginia, named Roger. As Nick slammed the Bible down on the table, Roger walked to the bars of his cell and spoke.

"I see you've been studying the Bible."

"No, not really." Nick said. "I was reading it, but it didn't seem to make much sense."

"Where did you start?" Roger asked.

"At the front of the book," Nick answered impatiently. "That's where you start reading any book."

"Not the Bible," Roger observed. "It's a series of books, and you should start with the New Testament. Try the Gospel of Matthew. You'll be able to relate to it better because it is more relevant to what you may have been taught as a child. It deals more directly with whatever problems you're facing right now."

Nick stared at Roger, wondering if he was crazy, but with a shrug of his shoulders, he reopened the Bible and found the Book of Matthew. Roger was right. Matthew was easier to understand and Nick continued reading. That afternoon, Nick read through Matthew, Mark, Luke, and John. He found all four Gospels exciting and meaningful. As he read through the Book of Acts and the Book of Romans, the Holy Spirit began leading him to a greater understanding. Nick was drawn closer to Calvary and began to see how Jesus was his Savior.

This guy, Jesus, he couldn't help thinking, *I've never paid much attention to Him, but he was a real stand-up guy. Why hasn't someone told me about Him before?*

One evening, just before lights out, Nick was reading the first chapter of the Book of Romans when the Holy Spirit let him feel a personal impact from the words Paul, the apostle, had written. It was an awakening for Nick's spirit because suddenly he could see how the words were meant for him.

"Because that, when they knew God, they glorified Him not as God, neither were they thankful: but vain in their imaginations, and their foolish heart was darkened." (Romans 1:21)

Tears of guilt welled up behind Nick's eyes as he continued reading. "Professing themselves to be wise, they became fools, and changed the glory of God into an image made like to corruptible man, and to birds, and fourfooted beasts, and creeping things.

"Wherefore God also gave them up to uncleanness through the lusts of their own hearts, to dishonor their own bodies between themselves:

"Who changed the truth of God into a lie, and worshiped and served the creature more than the Creator, who is blessed for ever. Amen." (Romans 1: 22-25)

Nick closed his eyes and let the meaning of these words sink into his soul. He was guilty of doing this very thing. He had been a fool while thinking he was the wisest of all men. He had dishonored himself and Gretchen with the lusts of his heart, but a question popped into his mind. *If God is truly a greater power, why does He let people dishonor themselves?* Opening his eyes, he read the very next verse.

"For this cause God gave them up unto vile affections. . ." Nick's brain reeled under the impact of what Paul had written. It answered his question. *If God can give us up to vile affections,* Nick realized, *it must be His way of teaching us that we're responsible, and answerable, for our own actions.* This thought embedded itself in Nick's mind, and he became convicted by the power of the Holy Spirit and suddenly knew that God was alive in Jesus. Nick could feel the Holy Spirit filling his heart with a desire to know the Lord in a very personal way.

As the lights were turned out, Nick lay back on his bunk and closed his eyes again. His thoughts took him back in time and let him see Jesus nailed to the cross at Calvary. In his heart, Nick heard the Lord speak.

"I'm doing this for you, Nick."

In response, Nick cried out to God, recalling as many of his sins as he could remember. "I know I'm a sinner, and I believe that Jesus died for my sins. Please forgive me, Father. I cannot carry my guilt any longer. In repentance I beg for Your saving grace. Jesus is my Lord and Savior."

Something wonderful happened in his cell that night. Nick changed masters. He was no longer a slave to heroin and he began to see a new image of God. He was overwhelmed by a hunger for God's Word, and everything he'd read in the Bible suddenly was colored with deep personal meaning. He accepted Jesus as the Lord of his life and was washed in the blood of the Lamb. Like rivers of living water, it flowed over him, washing away all the garbage in his life. He felt clean and spotless as he faced himself. Knowing God had forgiven his sins, tears of joy streamed down his cheeks as he wept with a new heart and mind. He could hardly wait to tell Gretchen what had happened. He now agreed with her decision about not living together until they were married.

Gretchen, however, was fighting a spiritual battle of her own. Overwhelmed by a deep sense of fear and guilt, she was seeking spiritual perfection. She was positive that God would not accept her until she was spiritually perfect.

This is a common mistake among many immature Christians who firmly believe they must earn God's love. In reality, it's a judgemental mistake that many people make against themselves. As long as they retain their own unforgiveness, they find it impossible to believe God has forgiven them. This leads them to the fallacy of believing they can earn their salvation by doing things that will make them spiritually perfect.

Gretchen was hungry for God's salvation and love. She knew Jesus was the Lord, but she didn't know her salvation was a free gift of God's grace, and couldn't be earned—it was given because He loved her. This truth she still had to learn, and it would elude her until she could forgive herself.

Searching for this truth, she attended a different church service every Sunday. She became confused as she wandered from one denomination to another without staying long enough to learn truth from any of them. Gretchen was actually fighting a battle within herself, driven by a need to know more about God and frustrated by her lack of understanding. She wanted everyone to know about Jesus, but she still hadn't met Him on a personal basis herself.

As a rebellious child she had rejected her mother's faith, and now she was confronted by the knowledge that she had been wrong. This added to her profound feeling of guilt and made it even more difficult to accept the truth she sought with the spirit of self-forgiveness needed for her own peace of mind. In an attempt to override this deep-seated sense of frustration, Gretchen adopted the zeal of an evangelist. She tried to impress everyone she met with the necessity of knowing and following Jesus.

An important part of her drug rehabilitation program was the admission that she was an addict and wanted help. Under the guidance of her counselor, an intelligent, young Jewish man named Aaron, Gretchen extended this admission to include all the sins that burdened her heart. Instinctively, she seemed to understand the healing nature of confession, but found herself confessing the same sins over and over again in a form of witness to Aaron. Subconsciously, Gretchen wanted Aaron to confess his sins and join her in following Jesus.

"Why," he asked with mounting impatience, "is it so important that I believe like you?"

Gretchen had read the four Gospels. Although she didn't completely understand them, she knew the truth was in the Bible somewhere, and what little she did comprehend she threw back at him.

"Because Jesus was the Lord of us all. He died for our sins."

"Gretchen," Aaron countered, "you speak of Jesus so glowingly. Wasn't he just a mortal? So he died for our sins—he's dead, now, isn't he?" Smiling to soften the impact of his questions, he added, "I know what you're trying to express and I want you to continue reaching for a better understanding of God because you need His strength and help, but please leave me out of it."

Aaron's statement and questions spoke directly to Gretchen's dilemma. She had used the past tense. Unknowlingly, he had stimulated her brain with a driving force that demanded an answer. Locking her eyes on his, and projecting a degree of confidence she really didn't feel, she replied, "Jesus died on the cross. He was buried, and after three days in the tomb, He rose again."

No longer smiling, Aaron asked, "What kind of sacrifice is that? If a man dies, knowing he will rise again in three days, is it really a sacrifice?" His smile returned. "Please don't misunderstand me," he added, "I believe in God. He is the Father of us all, and each of us, in our own way, must obey His laws. I have found my God and now you must find yours."

Gretchen left her counseling session that day

with Aaron's questions echoing in her brain. She was convinced the true answers were in the Bible, but even as she read God's Word, the answer continued to elude her. The more she read, the less sense it seemed to make. She was striving to make herself perfect for God, but nothing she read confirmed her purpose. Finally in desperation, one Friday night, she gave the problem to Jesus in prayer.

"God," she prayed, kneeling beside her bed, "You're crazy! I cannot be perfect. Unless You do something in my life, I'm either going to kill myself or go back to doing drugs. This is the worst I've ever felt in my life. Nothing makes any sense, and if Jesus is the Lord, let me feel Him in my heart because I've got to do something with my life and I can't go on like this." Feeling as if a burden had been lifted from her slender shoulders, Gretchen crawled into bed and fell asleep almost immediately.

As a surviving child of a disabled World War I veteran, she was eligible for educational benefits through the Veterans Administration. Gretchen used part of these benefits when she enrolled in acting classes, earlier. Aaron had encouraged her to go back to school, and she had an appointment at the V.A. office in Miami the following Monday. When she awoke on Saturday, following her desperate prayer, Gretchen felt a great sense of peace about herself and what she was planning to do. She didn't know what she wanted to study in school, but she knew this was the direction she should take for her future.

At the V.A. office on Monday, Gretchen was told to wait for the next available benefit officer for her interview. As she waited, various study possibilities ran through her mind. *I could always go back to acting,* she thought, *but that doesn't really excite me any more. Perhaps I should consider bookkeeping and accounting. With my drug history, I don't suppose I'd be accepted for nurse's training—they have access to controlled substances and if any turned up missing, I'd be blamed. Maybe I should just go with the flow, start back to school and see what develops.* She reached this conclusion just as her name was called. Entering the interviewer's office, she promised herself, *I'll be up front with this guy and tell him where I'm coming from. Maybe he'll have some ideas for me to think about.*

After a few basic questions and a review of Gretchen's V.A. file containing the record of her previous benefit usage, the officer asked, "What kind of school are you planning to enter?"

Gretchen answered by telling him about her drug addiction and how she was progressing in her rehabilitation. She explained how God was helping her win the fight and how she wanted to learn more about Jesus. "But," she concluded, "I need to learn how to make a living, so I suppose that should be my first consideration."

He smiled his understanding before saying, "I attended seminary myself, for a couple of years before changing the direction of my education. Have you thought of going to Bible college? With your background and personal experience in drug addiction, you might find a ministry in that field where spiritual help is so desperately needed."

God had answered her prayer. He'd made her wait for this particular man, someone who could relate to the direction she suddenly wanted to go. She let the warm feeling of this revelation sweep over her as she observed, "There's a Bible college in Hollywood Beach."

"If they'll accept you," he said, "I'll get your application approved for your government benefits and you'll be all set. The Florida Bible College is an excellent school. It could get you started on a whole new life."

In her heart, Gretchen was positive that God had

finally taken a direct hand in her life. A marvelous feeling of exaltation seemed to fill her with excitement. "I'll drive up to Hollywood Beach today and get an application," she declared. "I'll let you know as soon as I hear from them and I'll bring you the papers you'll need for approval."

Feeling very good about herself, Gretchen left the V.A. office and drove north to Hollywood Beach. Attempting to be perfect for God, she had given up wearing makeup and stylish clothes. In her dowdiness, she looked much older than her actual age, but she was proud of the *sacrifices* she'd made. She eagerly anticipated seeing how the female students at the college managed to achieve their perfection. *I'll fit right in,* she silently exulted. *Everyone will be plain and honest about their appearance. There will be no wicked lipstick, sinful eye shadow, low necklines, short skirts, sheer nylon stockings or fancy jewelry. Everyone will be modest, humble and devoted to God through study and deep contemplation. They won't be concerned about worldly things. Everything will be spiritual and perfect.*

As she parked the car and walked toward the Registrar's office, two girls with books under their arms passed her. They were dressed in brightly colored plaid skirts, both wearing nylons and low-heeled pumps. Their sweaters fit perfectly, neither tight nor baggy, revealing their femininity, and their lips glowed with a light, wet-looking, pink gloss.

They must be visitors, she thought, entering the building. *I'm sure they're not students.* Watching two boys join the girls, take their books and continue walking with them, she assumed, *Of course, those girls are here to see the boys. They were even carrying the boys' books.*

Entering the Registrar's office, Gretchen was greeted by a very attractive, older woman. She, too, was wearing makeup and her hair was set in a

167

fashionable manner. Her dress, stockings and shoes gave her the appearance of a successful business-woman. This surprised Gretchen, and she was about to ask for someone connected with the college when the woman spoke.

"May I help you?"

"I'd like to speak to the Registrar."

"I'm Mrs. Smith," the woman responded. "How may I serve you?"

"I'm Gretchen Martz, and I'd like to enroll as a student."

"Excellent," Mrs. Smith acknowledged warmly, bending slightly and reaching under the counter. "Let me give you a college catalog and registration forms." Indicating a table across the room, she added, "You may sit over there and fill them out. Do you need a pen?"

"May I take them home and bring them back later?" Gretchen asked.

"Certainly, my dear," was the reply, "but the next semester begins in two weeks. I'll need them back for consideration by Wednesday morning. We'll also need time to get transcripts from your former schools, so you'll have to act fast if you're thinking of starting immediately. You can send them in and we'll notify you."

Accepting the catalog and papers, Gretchen assured Mrs. Smith she'd have them back on time, thanked her for her courtesy, and left the office. Standing beside the car, she looked around. *These people,* she thought, *can't possibly know the Lord. They're not perfect. All the women are wearing makeup and nail polish, and they have ribbons or other decorations in their hair. What kind of Bible college is this?* Looking beyond the people, she admired the beauty of the campus and was impressed by the chapel. *I'll have to study their catalog and see what they say about themselves,* she silently concluded. *Maybe this is where God wants me to become perfect for Him.*

Gretchen spent the rest of the day poring over the catalog. The more she read, the more convinced she became that it was the school for her. Opening the application, she began filling it out.

Most of the required information was routine, but one section of the application made Gretchen stop and think. They wanted her to briefly state her personal relationship with the Lord. After much soul searching, she realized that she didn't know Jesus on a personal basis. She couldn't testify that He had directly influenced her life. What she eventually wrote made it obvious she didn't know much about the Lord, but equally obvious that she was seeking the Savior and wanted more knowledge of Him.

When it was finally completed, Gretchen sealed the application in the envelope the school had provided, stamped it, and walked to the corner mailbox. The moment it was posted and she could not withdraw it, her mind was flooded with negative thoughts.

You're a fool, her brain told her. *You'll never make it at that school. You haven't the money you'll need. You don't have the intellect for it. You've been out of school too long and you've forgotten how much you hated going to school.* She listened to this voice in her head, knowing it was her own voice, but was unable to discern the source of her negative thinking. She felt as if she were mocking herself and this was something she'd never done before. She didn't know, yet, that Satan is the father of lies and perfectly capable of feeding her brain false and negative thoughts.

The following Friday, Gretchen received notification that she had been accepted as a full time student by the Florida Bible College. For a moment, she experienced joy and exaltation, then serious doubts about her ability crowded out her initial happiness. Needing some kind of confirmation that she was doing the right thing, she called her Jewish counselor on Saturday morning.

"Aaron!" she exclaimed, "I've applied for college acceptance and it has been approved."

"Is it a good school?" he asked.

"It's the Florida Bible College in Hollywood Beach."

"Excellent," he said. "I've heard it's a fine school. Have you told Nick what you're planning to do?"

"Not yet," she responded. "I'm going to visit him at the jail this afternoon. I'll tell him then."

"Don't let him talk you out of it," Aaron advised. "I think it's the best thing you can possibly do for yourself."

"Orientation is tomorrow morning," she told him, "and I'm excited about going now that I've talked to you."

"Ah yes," he concluded, "a good Christian school should always start their teaching process on a Sunday. Go with God, my dear, and if I can help at any time, don't hesitate to call me again."

Aaron's encouragement was all that Gretchen needed. She didn't know how Nick would react to her news, but felt he'd be pleased with her decision. *I love him so much,* she thought, *and I know he loves me, so my going to Bible college will make him as happy as it's making me.* Thinking of their love she took comfort in the fact that Nick had been divorced for almost two years. *Perhaps,* she hoped, *with God's help, now we can be married, and when Nick is released from jail, we can serve our Lord together.*

LOVING ONE ANOTHER

*"A new commandment I give unto you,
That ye love one another, as I have loved you,
that ye also love one another."*

Jesus
(John 13:34)

Gretchen had written to Nick, telling him of her plan for salvation and explaining her need for spiritual and physical perfection. She was encouraged when he wrote back, "I know what you mean. I've already trusted the Lord."

The first words Nick spoke when Gretchen met him at the jail were, "I've been reading the Bible and now I understand! Jesus is the Lord!"

"Praise God!" she exclaimed. "You're learning about Jesus too!"

Feeling a new degree of unity and love, they told each other how God was acting in their lives. Nick beamed his approval when Gretchen mentioned Bible college. He explained how God had opened his eyes and heart to the Scriptures so that the Bible no longer confused him. Her happiness was obvious as she cheered his victory. They spent the entire visiting hour talking about Jesus and sharing the love they felt for Him and each other. They even prayed together when Gretchen said, "I'm going to orientation at the college chapel tomorrow."

"My probation hearing is coming up with Judge Futch in a few days," Nick said, "and I'm praying that

God will go with me."

"I'm in agreement with you on that," Gretchen offered. "Wouldn't it be wonderful if we could go to Bible school together?"

"That's not likely," Nick grinned, "but it sure won't hurt to let God know what we'd like to do, so let's pray for that, too."

This was the beginning of their walk with the Lord. Nick went back to his cell, happy with Gretchen's confirmation of his new understanding and her agreement with him regarding their future relationship. Gretchen felt a growing joy in her heart as she left the jail, knowing that Nick was in harmony with her feelings about God. They both had miles to go, but the journey had begun.

She realized they had done everything they possibly could to destroy the love they shared. How it had managed to survive the horror of their addiction to heroin and the violence it had caused was a complete mystery to her. The wonder of it amazed her until she considered another possibility. *God gave us this love for each other,* she suddenly understood, *and only He can take it away!* This was the thought Gretchen carried with her to the college orientation meeting on that fateful Sunday evening.

Sunday morning, she awoke with doubt back in her mind. The voice in her head was saying, *You're a wicked sinner and God hates you. You're not perfect. The people at that college are going to see you for what you really are and they're going to reject you.* Gritting her teeth, Gretchen ignored the voice and started preparing herself for the meeting.

Determined to make the right impression, she bathed and scrubbed her delicate skin almost raw before dressing as modestly as possible. She brushed her hair neatly, but used absolutely no makeup. *When I walk into that chapel tonight,* she told herself, *I'm going to look pure and perfect even if it kills me.* In spite of all this, she still felt guilty of sin as she drove over to the college.

Loaded with doubt and self-condemnation, she sat in the car outside the chapel and almost decided to forget the meeting and go back home. The voice in her head was strangely silent, allowing her to hear the voice in her heart. *Gretchen,* that voice whispered, *come to Me. I love you.* Getting out of the car, she slowly walked up the path to the chapel.

Entering the building, Gretchen experienced her first *miracle.* Everyone was pleased to see her. She was welcomed by friendly smiles and asked to sit in the front row. Looking around, she was impressed by the joy she saw in their eyes, but the voice in her head whispered, *They don't know you. They think you're as good as they are, but when they find out how you've lived in sin with Nick and used drugs, they'll run you off.* She was near tears when a tall, dignified older man strode to the pulpit and started to speak.

"I want to welcome all of you to Florida Bible College," he said, "but before we begin our orientation, let us pray and ask God's guidance in our lives." Bowing his head, he continued, "Dear Lord, we come to You this evening, trusting in Your great love, to dedicate our hearts and souls to Your glory. We know we're sinners and unworthy of that love, but we humbly beg You to take us as we are and guide us to a greater knowledge of You and to help us understand Your will and purpose in our lives. We ask this in the name of Your blessed Son, our Lord Jesus, who lived and died that our sins could be forgiven and was resurrected as proof of everlasting life. Amen."

Tears were streaming down Gretchen's cheeks as she looked up from that prayer and whispered her own "Amen." The voice in her heart murmured, *I love you, Gretchen. I know you and I love you. What you've done in the past is gone. There is no spot in you. Your sins have been forgiven. Rejoice and sin no more. Let your beauty shine for My glory and be the woman I created you to be.* In that instant, she knew without doubt that Jesus was alive in her heart. She had become a *born-again* Christian and the foolish kind of perfection she'd been seeking was no longer her objective. God loved her in spite of her sinful past.

As she listened to the orientation speakers and watched the reaction of those around her, Gretchen was overwhelmed by a deep sense of peace and understanding. She freely admitted she was unworthy of God's love and accepted it as a gift of grace which she could never earn by anything she could do. Filled with the warm glow of this divine love, she firmly resolved to follow the Lord and obey His commandments, and prayed that Nick would be inspired to do the same. She knew he was faced with a different kind of judgement in the person of Judge Futch. She understood quite clearly that as she was attending Florida Bible College, Nick was involved in a spiritual retreat within himself.

The Holy Spirit was guiding Nick through the Scriptures, and each day's reading was expanding his understanding of God's Word. His attitude and personal conduct underwent dramatic changes as God lifted his bitterness and filled him with a peace that overruled his dominating hatred for all forms of authority. He, too, had become a *born-again* Christian overflowing with the joy of God's forgiving love.

The change in Nick was apparent to the other inmates at the jail. It was so apparent that they suspected he had a secret stash of drugs, and many begged him to share it with them.

"Hey, man," one of them pleaded, "you're always high. Why don't you share your reefer with us? Let us have some of that good stuff you've been keeping to yourself."

Grinning with pleasure, Nick held up his Bible.

"This is what I'm using and I'll be glad to share it."

"Aw come on, Nick," the man responded, "I'm talking about the real stuff, not something printed in a book."

"This is the real stuff," Nick insisted. "It's the best there is and if you really want to get *high* there's plenty to go around."

"You're putting me on," the man growled. "I know you and I know where you came from so don't try to pull that *holy-Joe* stuff with me. You're the king of the junkies and your *old lady* is keeping you supplied, so don't give me any of that *jailhouse preacher* crap."

"Look, Emmett," Nick reasoned, "if you know me as well as you think you do, you know I don't fool around." Nick wasn't grinning as he added, "Jesus is the Lord and He's the answer. You're stuck in this jail with time on your hands. Why don't you give Jesus a chance? We can study the Bible together. You've got nothing to lose and everything to gain. If you want to get *high* with me, then open your heart and take a *hit* of God's Word."

"Okay, okay," Emmett said, half in disgust. "I've got nothing better to do, so I'll string along with you just to prove that you're wrong! God isn't interested in men like you and me. He wants *church-people,* not jailbirds. He wants good people and that doesn't include you or me, but if it'll make you happy, I'll take a *shot* of God with you."

That's how Nick's *jailhouse* Bible study class got started, and God honored it. In addition to Emmett, ten other men joined the group over the next four weeks. Without knowing it, Gretchen helped to accomplish this. Every afternoon, she would come to the jail and sit on the grass outside the broken, second-floor window of Nick's cell and loudly read Scripture to him. In effect, she was reading to the entire jail population on that side. They all heard what

175

she read and listened attentively as Nick responded from his Bible. This is how God used the training she was getting, both to strengthen Nick's faith before the date of his court appearance, and to plant a seed in other minds and hearts.

As that date approached, Nick found himself getting more and more involved in the Word of God. He discovered the teaching power of his marvelous radio voice and enjoyed using it to bring a better understanding to other men. This gave Nick a new degree of satisfaction that he hadn't been able to attain with all his drugs, money, or violence. The Holy Spirit was showing him a better way to achieve the happiness he'd been seeking in all the wrong places. Nick was receiving the infilling of God's love and being shown the real purpose for his life.

One afternoon, as Nick sat by the broken window in his cell listening to Gretchen read from the Scriptures what she'd studied that day at college, God provided an answer to his latest, and most pressing, question.

Unbeknown to Gretchen, Nick had been struggling to understand the concept of life after death. In the back of his mind, he felt that death was being used as a threat against sinners to force them into being good. He couldn't understand the premise of force in relation to God's forgiveness of sin by grace alone. As Gretchen read verses 28 and 29 from the 5th chapter of John's Gospel, Nick received a better understanding of life after death and resurrection from the grave. The words Jesus spoke hit him with great impact.

"Marvel not at this," Jesus said, "for the hour is coming, in which all that are in the graves shall hear His voice, And shall come forth: they that have done good, unto the resurrection of life; and they that have done evil, unto the resurrection of damnation."

Gretchen kept on reading, but Nick's brain was

digesting what he'd just heard. *Life after death wasn't the question,* he suddenly realized. *Everyone would have life after death. The question was how each of us would spend that eternal life. Would it be in the everlasting pain of damnation? Or would it be in the glory, peace and love of God?*

Using the gift of wisdom he'd received from the Holy Spirit, Nick pressed this new understanding a step further. *My life, and the way I live it, is actually my personal judgement day. What I have done, what I'm doing now, and what I will do in the future are the things Jesus will judge when He comes again in His glory.* Suddenly, the parable of the *workers in the vineyard* (Matthew 20:1-16) took on new meaning. The reward for the last man hired near the end of the day was the same as for the first man hired early in the morning. That reward was God's forgiveness and salvation, and regardless of when we seek it, it will be given.

By judging myself and admitting all my sins, he realized, *I can be forgiven. If I'm honest with myself and hold back nothing that I have done, I will not be judged a sinner.* The words Paul had written to the Corinthians confirmed this. "For if we judge ourselves we should not be judged." (1 Corinthians 11:31) This thought was foremost in Nick's mind as he prepared himself for his date in court with Judge Futch.

When that day finally arrived, the new Nick was apprehensive about what he should say and do in court. Gretchen quietly supported him in prayer throughout the hearing. His attorney prepared Nick's defense by gathering several character witnesses to testify to the changes in Nick's personality. There was no question as to his guilt, but it was hoped the judge would consider the changes and give Nick a chance to prove them. Judge Futch, however, was of a different mind.

As the hearing got underway, Nick's attorney

announced his intention of introducing his witnesses. Futch immediately voiced his opposing opinion. To say the least, he wasn't impressed.

"This is a waste of the court's time," Futch declared. "I know these witnesses are going to say a lot of good things about your client, but I already know Mr. Barbetta. He's been in my court before and there's nothing your people can say that'll change his record."

Faced with this judicial statement, the attorney leaned over to Nick and whispered, "You've got one shot at this."

"What is it?" Nick pressed.

"You can take the stand on your own behalf. It's your only chance to reach this judge and change his opinion of you."

"Okay, let's do it."

Nick was sworn in, but before the attorney could make any kind of introductory statement, Futch asked, "What would you like the court to do with you?"

"Your honor," Nick replied, "I would like the court to reinstate my probation with strict supervision. I'll submit to regular urine tests, outpatient therapy, drug programs or anything else the court wants me to do."

"You've said all that before," Futch stated grimly, "and you can forget it this time. You're going to prison. That's where you belong and that's what I'm going to order."

"Your honor," Nick countered, "you asked what I wanted and I'd like to go back out on probation. If you incarcerate me, you can only incarcerate my body because Jesus has already set me free. I've been locked up for the past six months, and in that time, I've learned the truth about a lot of things." He looked the judge right in the eyes. "Jesus said the truth shall set you free, and I have learned the ultimate truth. Jesus died and paid for my sins. He is my Savior and He has set me free!"

Futch silently studied Nick for several minutes. He

glanced through some papers on his desk. Looking up finally, he said, "I was prepared to sentence you today, but I'm going to postpone your sentencing for two weeks. I'm aware of what you've been doing in the jail," his eyes rested on Gretchen, "and I've heard about the broken window conversations you've had with your lady friend. I'm going to investigate your activities and check out your claimed change of attitude." Looking at the attorney, he announced, "You'll be notified of Mr. Barbetta's next appearance in this court."

Ten days later, Nick was conducting a Bible study class in the jail. He was leading a discussion of the 15th chapter of Luke's Gospel, the parable of the prodigal son. Nick had just explained how the father had divided his wealth and given a portion to one of his sons, when Judge Futch and two other men entered the room and sat down behind him. Nick knew someone was there, but didn't look back to see who. He continued the teaching.

"And not many days after, the younger son gathered all together, and took his journey into a far country, and there wasted his substance with riotous living.'" Looking up from the Bible, Nick expanded on this, saying, "In one way or another, each of us has done this very thing. We know what riotous living is all about, and we also know that it doesn't go on forever because there is a price each of us has had to pay. This next verse speaks to that point.

"'And when he had spent all, there arose a mighty famine in that land; and he began to be in want,'" Nick read. "Each of us knows what that verse means, don't we?"

The men in the class all nodded.

"When we've been in want," Nick continued, "we've been willing to do anything to get what we needed. In a large measure, that's why we're all in this jail, isn't it?"

They nodded again.

Nick led them on through the parable, explaining each verse, and when he came to the end of the story, he concluded with a summary of the parable's meaning. "Even though the older brother had remained faithful to the father, the younger son was honored and forgiven because he confessed his sins to the father. Where the one son had been dead to the family, he was once again alive because he'd seen the mess he'd made of his life and returned with a humble heart. This same welcome is awaiting each of us with our Father in heaven if we will come to Him and admit our sins. We can be free, and stay free with our Father's love, if we accept his forgiveness and follow Him."

Nick had been so engrossed in what they were studying that he hadn't heard the visitors leave the room. When he turned to see who was there, only three empty chairs faced him. The men in the class told him who had come to hear him teach. Nick thanked Jesus for giving him the opportunity to be a good witness of God's forgiveness. He wasn't certain what kind of impression he'd made on the judge, but he felt good about how the Lord had led him to do the teaching. Judge Futch didn't let him ponder this for very long. Nick was called back into court the following day.

"Nick," the judge said, "I don't know why I keep fooling with you, but somehow I feel you've really gotten onto something positive this time. You've impressed me and some of your other judges with what you're doing in the jail. You've violated your probation with me and another judge, but we both agree that maybe, just maybe, you deserve another chance. Have you got anything to say for yourself?"

Not only did Nick have something to say for himself, but he used the opportunity to give a strong Christian witness to everyone in court that morning.

With the Holy Spirit giving him inspiration to speak, Nick told them how he'd been set free from his addiction to heroin and how he wished to serve God for the rest of his life.

At the conclusion of his witness, Judge Futch ordered the reinstatment of his probation and released him with a warning. "This is your last chance. If you mess up just one more time, I'm going to put you away for a very long time. I'm going to follow your probation and you'll be back here in this court if I get one even little negative report on your behavior. Is that clearly understood?"

"Yes, your honor," Nick replied. "I understand and with Jesus in my heart, I'll make it this time."

After being dismissed, Nick left the courtroom with a wise, knowing grin on his face. Gretchen was waiting for him and he knew exactly what he wanted to do the moment he was free.

**Gretchen and Nick fell more in love
with Jesus as their Lord.**

A MORE PERFECT UNION

"For whosoever shall do the will of my Father which is in heaven, the same is my brother, and sister, and mother."

Jesus
(Matthew 12:50)

A royal kinship, having nothing to do with salvation, is available to everyone. It is a matter of free choice, and every person on earth makes that choice—although many of us make it without understanding its true impact. This was the case with Gretchen and Nick.

Nick had celebrated his 26th birthday and Gretchen was just 15 when they met. God gave them a love for each other that couldn't be destroyed. Without intending its destruction, they did everything possible to violate and crush the love. In this subconscious effort, they failed. They chose to follow the *dark master,* and in his service they became addicted to heroin, gave themselves over to moral corruption, committed crimes of almost every description and wallowed in the weakness of the flesh. They surrendered their human dignity, honor and pride to a very demanding master, believing they were serving themselves. The payment they received was unworthy of the love they'd been given. They surrendered that love and themselves to the master of Hell without being aware of the choice they'd made.

George Meyer, Al Capone's "Devil Driver", put it

this way, "You freely choose your master and you're rewarded accordingly. The first sixty-six years of my life were spent as a slave of Satan and he paid me well with pain, disgrace and incarceration. Hell does exist and Satan is alive. Those of you who are presently guests in his castles here on earth surely can recognize his insane laughter at your misery. The slam of heavy steel doors and the creeping hand of homosexuality punctuate his hospitality. I spent 31 years in his castles before I learned the truth and accepted the saving grace of God's love."

When Jesus said, "He that is not with me is against me; and he that gathereth not with me scattereth abroad," (Matthew 12:30) He drew the line between the two choices each of us has to make for himself. When Nick read those words, he immediately saw the mistake he'd made and resolved to correct it. Gretchen had come to the same understanding, and when she met him outside the jail, they took the first small step toward forming a more perfect union in the love God had given them.

During those last few months in jail, the change in Nick was an observable miracle. Prior to this, his reputation on the outside had been established by the quality of dope he could supply his dealers. Everyone knew he always had the very best dope. This time outside, he wanted to maintain that reputation by sharing a vastly superior product.

I'm going to be a distributor of the truth, Nick planned. *God's Word is the answer to everything, and I'm going to take it to the heart and mind of all those who need the salvation of God's love.*

Gretchen arranged for the college to send Nick correspondence courses while he was inside. These courses guided his Bible study and showed him the most effective way to share his testimony with fellow inmates. When he was released in March of 1977, Nick knew from experience the value of inspirational teaching, and knew that spiritual training could provide him with the information needed to be a servant of God. The miracle of his release was proof to him that Jesus wanted him to serve this way.

Nick had been facing 45 years of *hard-time*. His criminal record and previous probation violations stood in the way of his ever being set free. Judge Futch enjoyed the reputation of giving maximum punishment to all convicted felons, and as such, Nick was totally at his mercy. But with Jesus in his heart, Nick was sentenced to 15 years probation. He was assigned to a Jewish probation officer, a no-nonsense lady who understood the criminal mind and wouldn't tolerate a false spirit of religion. Nick established his degree of Christian commitment with her at their first meeting.

Sitting in her office, he said, "All things are possible with God."

"How do you mean that?" she asked.

"Last week I was sitting in my jail cell reading my Bible, without any hope of being free," he told her, "but as I read Psalm 142, twelve words in the seventh verse glowed in my eyes."

"Go on," she urged.

"David prayed," Nick continued, "'Bring my soul out of prison, that I may praise Thy name.' As I read these words, the Lord unlocked my heart and gave me hope and I prayed that Psalm for the next four days. I didn't know if the Lord would set me free, but I promised to give Him all the glory if He did."

"And how do you propose to do that?" she pressed.

"I am now praying the tenth verse of Psalm 143," Nick answered. "'Teach me to do Thy will; for Thou art my God: Thy spirit is good, lead me into the land of uprightness.' This is my prayer and I feel that God will honor it by showing me how He wants to be praised."

Fred Barbetta
was Nick's best man
at Gretchen and
Nick's Wedding.
Kathy, (driver
for the
quarter robbery)
was Gretchen's
Bride's Maid.

"What about your personal life," she asked, "how are you going to change that?"

"By getting straight with God and doing what's right."

"We'll see how that works out," she observed with a smile. "I'll give you a chance to prove yourself, but the first time you screw up, you're going back to jail. Is that clearly understood?"

Nick nodded as he said, "That's all I ask for. God will help me do the rest. I've put my trust in Him."

That same afternoon, Gretchen and Nick decided to get married. They wanted their lives to be joined with the Lord's blessing and both had confessed and repented the sin of their previous relationship. Nick felt a powerful calling to minister to prisoners. He didn't know how he could obey that assignment and still support a wife, but he was certain Jesus would show him the way. He also understood that his relationship with his mother and father had to be healed. With Gretchen beside him, he went to Hollywood for that purpose.

After telling his mother everything, he announced, "Gretchen and I are going to get married. We're planning our wedding and we want you and Dad to come."

"When?" she asked.

"In two weeks," he answered.

"Nick," she said, "you just got out of jail and you don't have a job. What are you getting married on and how are you going to live?"

"We're going to do this on faith," he replied. "The Lord will provide all that we need."

"Please," she suggested, "talk this over with some other people. Get their opinions and advice. Listen to what they say and be certain you're doing what God wants you to do, before rushing into anything."

They accepted this suggestion and Gretchen

took Nick over to the college where she introduced him to the people she knew. As believing Christians, with Jesus in their hearts, they prayed together, asking the Lord to guide them. The president of the college voiced his concern with one simple question.

"Do you both know Jesus Christ?"

"Yes," they answered sincerely. "He is our Savior and the Lord of our lives."

By the end of the day, they were firmly convinced that God had spoken to them through the people they'd seen. Their desire to be married had been confirmed by everyone they'd met and the college president offered to conduct the ceremony in his home. This was the final confirmation they were seeking. With joy in their hearts, Nick and Gretchen set the date. Nick knew he needed a job, so he applied at a lumber yard.

Facing the owner of the yard, he asked, "I'm wondering if you need any help?"

The man looked him up and down before answering, "No, we don't need anyone right now, but I'll give you an application and we'll keep it on file." Pointing toward the end of the counter, he added, "You can fill it out over there and let me look at it when you're finished."

Nick glanced at the form and saw the question: "Have you ever been arrested?" He grinned as he saw they'd only left one inch of space for the answer. He would need at least a full page for a true answer.

"Look," he said to the man, "before I fill this out, I've got something to tell you."

"Then tell me."

Nick felt the Lord in his heart as he opened his mouth to speak. "I'm an ex-junkie," he confessed. "I just came out of jail. I've been shooting dope for years and I'm out on 15 years probation. I just came out, but I'm a different person from when I went in. I've received Jesus Christ as my Savior and He's changed my life. The old Nick Barbetta, the guy I used to be, is dead. I'm a new man now and I want to serve the Lord."

The man reached out and grabbed the application from Nick's hand. *That's it,* Nick thought, *this guy doesn't want a jailhouse Christian working here.*

"Mr. Barbetta," the man said, "I haven't ever had anyone be so up front with me before." He smiled. "If you really want a job, be here at 7:00 o'clock tomorrow morning and we'll have one for you."

Nick worked at the lumber yard for two weeks, but right after the wedding the Lord made another change in their lives. The wedding was beautiful, attended by both of his parents, with his father as best man. Gretchen's mother and many of her friends also witnessed the marriage. The ceremony was held on a Wednesday. Gretchen attended her classes on Thursday and Friday, and they honeymooned at Disneyworld that weekend. On their return, Nick was offered a job by the pastor of the Westside Baptist Church in Hollywood.

He'd met Pastor Jim Pollard in jail. Pollard was familiar with Nick's background and had observed the change in him while ministering to the other prisoners. He was impressed with Nick's sincerity and purpose. An ex-con himself, Jim Pollard knew how the Lord could deal with prisoners and understood Nick's desire to reach other men in prison. Under Pastor Pollard's guidance, the Westside Church had established a halfway house for ex-cons. Nick was offered the directorship of *Active House.* It was his first official organized ministry and he accepted the job with a happy heart.

"This is what I've been praying for!" Nick told the pastor.

In this capacity, he found himself working with the probation and parole departments of local law enforcement agencies. His own probation officer was among them. One day, after an official visit to the house, she faced Nick with the reality of their professional relationship.

"Look," she said with a smile, "this is ridiculous. I keep forgetting that you're one of my clients. I'm always calling you for advice on what I should do with many of my other clients, yet you're still on probation yourself."

"I don't have any problem with that," Nick volunteered, "and I've still got lots of time left on my probation."

"I know how you feel, Nick, but we're going to have to get you off this *paper* time. I'm going to write your judges and see if they can't cut you loose from the rest of your 15 years."

One of the judges simply signed a release, but the other one, Judge Futch, wanted to know what was going on. He wanted details, so she and Nick went to see him together.

"What's this all about?" Futch asked. "Normally a probation officer comes to me requesting that I put someone back in prison. This is the first case I've had of being asked to release a man from his probation. What's going on here?"

She explained what Nick was doing and told him how much she valued Nick's help and advice. Futch questioned Nick in great detail about his activities and associates. This gave Nick an excellent chance to witness about the changes in his life, and his probation officer confirmed everything he said.

Futch signed the release and Nick was completely free. His life of crime and degradation was over. Gretchen had started her own ministry out of the college. She was active in the Youth Detention Center and Nick joined her in this work. With the stigma of his probation lifted, Nick also wanted to join her as a student at the Bible college, so this was his next move.

At the same time, Nick started going back to jail every Sunday with another man from their church. The guards knew Nick and had witnessed the change in his life, so they welcomed him and made arrangements for a small Sunday service in the jail library.

Only four men attended the first meeting, but when Nick announced their purpose, he got the complete attention of all four. "I'm going to show each of you how to be free," he told them. "Jesus Christ is your Savior and He'll set you free if you'll let Him."

The men nodded their interest.

"We're going to teach you about Jesus," Nick continued, "and ask you to teach the other inmates in the jail. When we come back next Sunday, I want each of you to bring another man with you—so make a friend in Christ and help the Lord help him."

Following this pattern of evangelism, the Sunday class rapidly grew in size. In four weeks, the library was crowded with inmates. After only two months, Nick and his friend had to schedule two classes every Sunday. This was Nick's first formal experience teaching adults, and it confirmed his calling. With Gretchen's encouragement, he started attending two college classes to expand his knowledge for his growing ministry. Jesus was using him to reach tormented souls and Nick was growing in his faith.

In addition to the halfway house, the Sunday ministry, and his college classes, Nick also took on a part-time counseling assignment with the same drug program that had helped Gretchen. He was overloading himself with voluntary obligations, but the joy he received in serving the Lord kept him going. He learned quickly that life in Christ can be very demanding and exciting, but the Lord was about to use his eagerness to teach him a valuable lesson. As a paid counselor in the drug program, Nick's actions were subject to secular regulations and administration. Secular rules do not always agree with Christian principles of conduct.

Right after breakfast one Saturday morning, Nick was helping Gretchen do the dishes when the phone rang. Hanging up his dish towel, he took the call. It was one of the young girls he'd been counseling in the program. She sounded depressed and upset.

"What's wrong, Nancy?" he questioned.

"I've come to the end," she murmured. "I can't take it any longer. Something has to give and I've got a whole bottle of pills."

"Now simmer down. It can't be that bad. Where are you?"

"I'm at home," she sobbed.

"Don't do anything foolish," Nick advised. "I'll be there in 15 minutes and we'll talk about it."

Nick spent a couple of hours with Nancy. When he left, she was at peace with herself and praising God for His forgiveness. Jesus had used Nick to keep her from killing herself and Nick felt justified in what he'd done to help her, but the girl's father didn't understand Nick's purpose and reported his visit to the program's director. Nick was called in to explain why he'd violated the rule about seeing a client outside the office.

"I'm sorry," Nick explained, "but Nancy was suicidal and I had to act fast."

"That's no excuse," he was told. "You should have reported her problem to the counseling staff and acted on their instructions. You had no business going to the girl's home. It's a direct violation of our regulations and it cannot be tolerated."

"Look," Nick reasoned, "she was planning to end her life. I could not just tell her, 'It's Saturday morning, Nancy, you'll have to wait until Monday when the office is open and you can come in and talk it over with me.' I went out and stopped her. That's what she needed and I gave it to her."

"It was wrong, Nick," the director said. "You violated our rules, so I've got to let you go."

When Nick told Gretchen he'd been fired, she broke into a bright smile and exclaimed, "Praise the Lord! Now you can go to college full time!"

He'd been resisting this because of the expense involved, but looking into her eyes, he grinned and said, "I'm through fighting God over this college thing. I'll go over with you on Monday and sign up for a full schedule. I'll just have to get a part-time job to earn the money we'll need."

"Nick," Gretchen reminded him, "we're in this together. I've got my classes handled, so I'll look for a part-time job also. The important thing is to get you started toward a full time ministry."

They both found work and Nick entered the Florida Bible College as a regular student. Gretchen was ahead of him in her studies and she graduated with a Bachelor's Degree in Biblical Education, with a minor in Theology. Nick stayed in school for three years before accepting God's calling to a ministry in Pennsylvania. He attended another Bible college for one semester, than quit his formal education and entered God's service on a full time basis.

After witnessing Nick's dedication and commitment to the Lord, the pastor of his church called him in for a career conference. He outlined a program of studies for Nick to follow and added, "When you complete this, I'll arrange for your ordination to the ministry."

"But I don't have a college degree," Nick said.

Smiling patiently, the pastor observed, "There's nothing in Scripture requiring a college degree from a Bible college. I'll help you prepare for ordination and we'll have you examined by a panel of ministers. When you gain their approval, God will honor your desire to serve and you will be ordained right here in our church."

Nick was ordained in 1982. He has never looked back. He and Gretchen are both ordained ministers in the family of God. Their ministry is prison-oriented and they serve full time as a team, taking the Lord's salvation into the prisons where Jesus can heal the hearts and minds of prisoners and set them free.

Nick ministering to a prisoner.

EPILOGUE

"I cried unto the Lord with my voice; with my voice unto the Lord did I make my supplication."

King David
(Psalms 142:1)

Gretchen was born with a restless spirit. As a young girl, she witnessed the protest against the war in Vietnam. She opened her heart to the questionable logic contained in the music of a troubled generation. Her imagination was stirred by role-models who reflected civil unrest and seemed to glorify rebellion against the policies of a different generation. She was also blessed with an active imagination that permitted her to escape reality by creating personal fantasies.

She found hope in her dreams of becoming an Olympic skater, only to have this fantasy smashed by the economics of running an ice skating facility in sunny Florida. In disappointment, she turned to the ruthless, self-indulgent, immature philosophy of the drug culture that was inspired by the music she loved. When she met Nick, Gretchen was already addicted to the attitude of "if it feels good, do it."

Nick's personality was the product of the violence he loved. Subconsciously, in his heart, he also harbored a fantasy. His dream was of physical power, power to demand obedience from others for his selfish satisfaction. He dreamed of becoming a recognized member of the Mafia and gaining the respect of the wealthy and powerful men he saw driving big cars and escorting beautiful ladies to expensive clubs. He flirted with this dream at the *Four O'clock Club* and gained some degree of notoriety through the pain he loved to inflict.

When God brought Gretchen and Nick together, neither of them recognized the love they were given as coming from Him. Jesus used that love to keep them within reach of their ultimate salvation, but He let them do everything possible to destroy that love before finding them with His greater love. He let them sink to the lowest possible point of human existence before taking them in His arms and setting them on the course He had planned for their lives.

Today Gretchen and Nick are married. God has provided them with a beloved adopted son, Justin Daniel. They share a prison ministry called CROSS ROADS and are led to share their lives and the love of God with inmates and anyone else who will listen. They also minister to young people, helping them avoid the pitfalls of drug addiction that they themselves experienced.

The CROSS ROADS PRISON MINISTRY is funded by churches and individuals who believe God wants to reach those behind bars. Chaplain Ray's International Prison Ministry has long emphasized the need for greater church and individual involvement with prison inmate rehabilitation. Chaplain Ray has often asked the question, "Which would you rather face on a dark street at night, an ex-con with Jesus in his heart, or an ex-con looking for the money he needs for a fix?" Christian commitment is the only answer that works, but it takes love and dedication to bring it to those who need it the most.

**Nick and Gretchen
Wedding Day 1977**

Gretchen, a helpmate and minister.

**Nick enjoys Justin Daniel,
his adopted son.**

**The Lord restores the years the
canker worm (heroin) ate.**

Justin is a joy to Gretchen